Salvation Songs
Seventy great hymns and their stories

By Mark Woods

© Mark Woods 2013

The rights of Mark Woods to be identified as the author
of this work have been asserted by him in accordance with the
Copyright, Designs and Patents Act 1988.

ISBN 978-1-907636-75-2

All rights reserved. No part of this publication may be reproduced or
transmitted in any form or by any means, electronic or mechanical,
including photocopying, recording, or any information storage and
retrieval system without permission in writing from the author.

Unless otherwise indicated, scripture quotations are from
The Holy Bible, English Standard Version® (ESV®),
copyright © 2001 by Crossway, a publishing ministry of Good News
Publishers. Used by permission. All rights reserved.

Published by Verité CM Ltd
Unit 2, Martlets Way, Goring Business Park, Goring by Sea,
West Sussex BN12 4HF
United Kingdom
email: enquiries@veritecm.com
web: veritecm.com

British Library Cataloguing Data
A catalogue record of this book is available from The British Library

Cover design, typesetting and production management by
Verité CM Ltd, West Sussex UK +44 (0) 1903 241975

Printed in England

For Kathy, with thanks

Contents

Foreword 8

Introduction 9

Ah, holy Jesus 11
All hail the power 14
All my hope on God is founded 17
All things bright and beautiful 20
And are we yet alive? 23
And can it be? 26
At even, ere the sun was set 29
Blest be the tie that binds 32
Break thou the bread of life 35
Breathe on me, breath of God 38
By gracious powers, so wonderfully sheltered 40
Christ is risen! Hallelujah! 42
Come down, O love divine 45
Come, let us sing of a wonderful love 47
Come, ye thankful people, come 50
Come, thou fount of every blessing 53
Creator Spirit, by whose aid 55
Dear Lord and Father of mankind 58
Eternal Father, strong to save 61
Father of mercies, in thy Word 64
Father, hear the prayer we offer 67

Fill thou my life, O Lord my God 69

For all the saints 72

Glorious things of thee are spoken 75

God of grace and God of glory 78

Great God, we sing thy mighty hand 80

Great is thy faithfulness 83

Guide me, O thou great Jehovah 85

Hail, thou once despised Jesus 87

Hail to the Lord's anointed 89

I need thee every hour 92

I'll praise my maker while I've got breath 94

Immortal, invisible, God only wise 97

In a byre near Bethlehem 99

It is a thing most wonderful 101

Jesus lives! 104

Jesus shall reign 106

Jesus, lover of my soul 108

Just as I am 111

King of glory, King of peace 114

Lead us, heavenly Father, lead us 117

Lord of all hopefulness 119

Love divine 121

Make me a channel of your peace 124

It came upon the midnight clear 126

My song is love unknown 129

Now thank we all our God 132

Now the green blade riseth 134

O come, O come, Immanuel 136

O, dearest Lord, thy sacred head 139

O God of Bethel 141

O little town of Bethlehem 144

O Love of God, how strong and true 147

O Love that wilt not let me go 150

O sacred head, sore wounded 152

O worship the King 155

Peace, perfect peace 157

Ride on, ride on in majesty 159

Rock of ages 162

Tell out, my soul 165

The day thou gavest, Lord, is ended 167

The light of the morning is breaking 170

There's a light upon the mountain 172

There's a wideness in God's mercy 175

Through the love of God our Saviour 178

We come unto our fathers' God 181

When I survey the wondrous cross 184

Where cross the crowded ways of life 186

Who would true valour see 189

About the author 192

Foreword

Most of this book was written as a series of articles for a church magazine resources website, www.thesheepdip.co.uk. They were an enjoyable monthly task over a period of several years. Some of them have also appeared in the *Methodist Recorder* and in the now-defunct *Baptist Times*.

Because of the nature of their composition there is some repetition, for instance when hymns by the same author are dealt with. Reviewing them as a whole, however, I was glad to find that there is surprisingly little, and most of what there was I have edited out.

I drew on a range of biographical and resources when I was preparing them. There are also several good websites, of which www.cyberhymnal.org is particularly useful.

Most older hymns exist in various forms. I have not tried to return to the originals as the efforts of successive editors have on the whole tended to improve them; in a rather arbitrary way I have stuck to the versions I know best.

Introduction

Which influences us more, the songs we sing or the sermons we hear? Ministers who spend hours preparing their weekly words of wisdom might hope it's the latter. In reality, though, it is probably the songs. Somehow, good words are given extra force by good music, and singing them with other people means that we are sharing very powerful ideas and emotions together.

The Anglo-Saxon Protestant tradition has given the Church some of its greatest congregational hymns. At their best, they feed the spirit and enrich the mind with the treasures of their authors' deep thinking and theological insight. Over the years they become part of our mental and spiritual furniture. They teach us how to be Christians without our realising it. At the end of our lives, when memory begins to fail, they are often as clearly remembered as ever they were. They are linked with our most intimate experiences of God.

Not all the hymns we love are good verse, and not all of them are good theology; though if a hymn has endured for a generation or two, there is usually a reason for it. Some of them are becoming unsingable, because they use words that are archaic or they have ceased to speak to a new generation. Some of these can be rescued with a bit of careful editing, but not all of them. In some cases it is best to let a hymn fade away with dignity.

Hymns always have been edited, and often for the better. Some of those we value today were rush jobs at the time, and later hands have given them some much-needed polish. There is no justification, though, for a wholesale attack on old-fashioned language just because it is old-fashioned. It is the strangeness of some of the words and phrases in these hymns, like the strangeness of the architecture of a cathedral, that makes them worshipful.

Over the last three or four decades there has been an explosion of new writing and a wide acceptance of new forms of worship. Songs from Taizé and the Celtic tradition have made their way into the mainstream. The hallmarks of the evangelical/charismatic tradition which has become so influential, though, have been songs which are either simple, personal and devotional, or triumphant assertions of God's power and majesty. It is wrong to say that they have no theology at all, but in general – though there are exceptions from writers like Matt Redman and Godfrey Birtill, for instance – they do not develop ideas in any particularly interesting way. That is not a criticism in itself; many of them are lovely to sing, they speak straight to the heart and it would be foolish not to use them and learn from them. I have not written about them simply because there is not much to say.

More recently, there has been a welcome move in these circles to recover the older tradition of hymn-writing. Stuart Townend and Keith Getty, for instance, have produced fine work which speaks to contemporary spirituality.

The 70 hymns about which I have written in this book were composed in different contexts. Most of them are from the four nations of the United Kingdom, though there are several from the United States and other countries. Some are ancient, translations from Latin originals.

As well as this, though, they were written by individuals who lived at a particular time and in a particular place. They were responding to the felt needs of their age and expressing their own experience of God, which was conditioned by what the people around them thought and believed, and how they expressed it. Hymns have roots, in other words; and while at one level they express the timeless truths of the Christian faith, at another they are much more local. One of things I have tried to do in this book is draw attention to those roots, where they help us understand why what we are singing was written, or why it was written in the way it was.

Above all, though, I have tried to show how the hymns speak to our minds and hearts. I have shed light, as best I can, on the flow of argument and inspiration which created them. Where I think it would help, I have added biblical references. I have written as a traditional Baptist pastor, whose concern is always to lead a congregation into a deeper knowledge of God.

Ah, holy Jesus, how hast thou offended,
That man to judge thee hath in hate pretended?
By foes derided, by thine own rejected,
O most afflicted.

Who was the guilty? Who brought this upon thee?
Alas, my treason, Jesus, hath undone thee.
'Twas I, Lord Jesus, I it was denied thee:
I crucified thee.

Lo, the Good Shepherd for the sheep is offered;
The slave hath sinned, and the Son hath suffered;
For our atonement, while we nothing heedeth,
God intercedeth.

For me, kind Jesus, was thy incarnation,
Thy mortal sorrow, and thy life's oblation;
Thy death of anguish and thy bitter passion,
For my salvation.

Therefore, kind Jesus, since I cannot pay thee,
I do adore thee, and will ever pray thee,
Think on thy pity and thy love unswerving,
Not my deserving.

Ah, holy Jesus

THE greatest hymns are those in which profound doctrine meets profound feeling and in which the skill of the writer combines with the power of the music to strike home in the mind and heart together. The English language has the richest treasury of hymns in the world, but even so not many manage to do this.

Ah, holy Jesus is one. Written by Lutheran pastor Johann Heermann (1585-1647), it is a profound meditation on the death of Christ, on responsibility, and on redemption. Above all, it is personal: for Heermann, Christ is a real human being who was betrayed by his closest friends, and he feels that injury profoundly. There is a note of grieving through the hymn which is only slightly lifted in the last verse. This is a hymn for Lent, for Good Friday: it is not for a time of cheerfulness. Sing it quietly, seated perhaps, with the simplest of musical arrangements.

The hymn plays throughout on the ironies of salvation, the paradoxes which have brought us to where we are. It is almost incredible that 'holy Jesus' should be afflicted in the way the gospels describe. In the second verse we admit responsibility. We, the singers, are on trial before a court. Christ is the witness; the judge asks, 'Who was the guilty? Who brought this upon thee?' From the dock we answer, 'I it was denied thee – I crucified thee.' Both theologically and devotionally, this is right. We are not Peter and the other disciples, but they represented us; in their place, any of us would have done the same.

So the hymn moves to explain the meaning of what happened, and the paradoxes continue. The Good Shepherd is offered for the sheep; the Son suffers for the slave; God works salvation for a human being, who 'nothing heedeth', who is indifferent to the sacrifice. But a note of wonder enters the hymn with the fourth verse – 'For me, kind Jesus, was thy incarnation ...' ('oblation' means 'offering'). There is a humble acknowledgement of Christ's love, not for the world – in some abstract, coldly correct theological statement – but for me, as a unique human being. The Lutheran Heermann is clear that we can contribute nothing to our own salvation – it all comes of unmerited grace.

> *Therefore, kind Jesus, since I cannot pay thee,*
> *I do adore thee, and will ever pray thee,*
> *Think on thy pity and thy love unswerving,*
> *Not my deserving.*

Heermann's life was lived in the shadow of the devastating Thirty Years' War (1618-48), which ravaged the states of what was to become Germany and left deep scars on the national psyche. It was also lived in the shadow of personal loss and illness. He had periods of ill-health from his early years; his first wife died, and his town, Köben, was ruinously plundered several times by Catholic troops, reducing him and his family to poverty. For the last 13 years of his life he was unable to preach, though he still wrote.

The English version we sing is by Robert Bridges, a skilful poet who wrote and translated several hymns.

The tune to which the hymn is sung is by Johann Cruger (1598-1662), Heermann's contemporary; it was borrowed by J S Bach for his *St Matthew Passion*. The five-note descent at the end of each stanza matches the sombre emphasis of the verses perfectly; it leaves us where Heermann would have wanted us to be, with the thought 'Not my deserving' echoing in our minds.

*A*ll hail the power of Jesus' name!
　Let angels prostrate fall;
Bring forth the royal diadem,
And crown him Lord of all.

Ye chosen seed of Israel's race,
Ye ransomed from the Fall,
Hail him who saves you by his grace,
And crown him Lord of all.

Sinners, whose love can ne'er forget
The wormwood and the gall,
Go spread your trophies at his feet,
And crown him Lord of all.

Let every kindred, every tribe
On this terrestrial ball,
To him all majesty ascribe,
And crown him Lord of all.

O that with yonder sacred throng
We at his feet may fall!
Join in the everlasting song,
And crown him Lord of all.

All hail the power

SOME traditional hymns are heavy on theology and light on joy. *All hail the power of Jesus' name* has both. It is steeped in biblical knowledge and underpinned by a solid hope in the Gospel. But there is also a cheerful lightness of touch about it; this is a hymn to be sung with gladness.

Edward Perronet, the author (1726-1792) was descended from Huguenot refugees who had settled in England. His father was an Anglican vicar and Perronet became a Methodist, working closely with John and Charles Wesley. Like many early Methodists, he suffered for his faith:

John Wesley wrote that Perronet was 'thrown down and rolled in mud and mire' in Bolton once.

He was rather in awe of Wesley, who once attempted to get him to preach in his place. Perronet announced that he would preach the greatest sermon ever preached, and proceeded to read the Sermon on the Mount.

He wrote three volumns of poetry, but *All hail the power* is the only one of his hymns to be regularly sung today. There are echoes of various texts within it. In Philippians 2. 9-11, for instance, Paul says that 'God exalted him to the highest place, and given him the name that is above every name, that at the name of Jesus every knee should bow ...' In Ephesians 1. 20-22 he writes that God seated Christ at his right hand, 'far above all rule and authority, power and dominion, and every title that can be given ...' In Colossians 1. 15 he says that Jesus is 'the image of the invisible God, the first-born over all creation'. The 'seed of Israel's chosen race' in verse 3 is from Romans 11. 5.

Most of all, there are echoes of Revelation. The angels in chapter 5 worship the Lamb; in chapter 7 the martyrs dressed in white robes sing, 'Salvation belongs to our God, who sits on the throne, and to the Lamb.'

The message of the hymn is that Jesus is King. It is not subtle verse, but it is not just a random assortment of texts, either. Perronet knew what he wanted to say. In the original version the hymn is much longer (like many from that era): if we were to sing it all, we would have 'Crown him, ye morning stars of light, who fixed this floating ball', and 'Hail him, ye heirs of David's line, whom David Lord did call,' among others. He wants to stress the absolute and unconditional Lordship of Christ. It is over Jews and Gentiles and over the whole created world, and everyone is called to bow down and acknowledge it; and if he has missed anyone out, there is a catch-all verse at the end – 'Let every kindred, every tribe/ On this terrestrial ball ...'

Interestingly, the last verse as we have it was added by John Rippon, the Baptist minister and hymn-book compiler, in 1787. He was a Calvinist, whose predecessor at the New Park Street chapel was John Gill, who preached a theology of limited atonement. Rippon might have found such a full-blooded call for a universal repentance a little hard to take. So, 'O that with yonder sacred throng/ We at his feet may fall' has the effect of shifting the emphasis of the hymn from Perronet's majestic, universal vision of Christ's lordship to the personal status before God of the individual believer. It is an expression of hope, rather than precisely of assurance.

It is a good last verse, but it is not the one Perronet wrote. Missing it out changes the meaning back again, and leaves us with a completely different emphasis.

All hail the power is usually sung to one of two wonderful tunes: *Diadem*, for congregations which are confidently musical, and *Miles Lane*, for those which are a little more sedate.

All my hope on God is founded;
He doth still my trust renew,
Me through change and chance he guideth,
Only good and only true.
God unknown, he alone
Calls my heart to be his own.

Pride of man and earthly glory,
Sword and crown betray his trust;
What with care and toil he buildeth,
Tower and temple fall to dust.
But God's power, hour by hour,
Is my temple and my tower.

God's great goodness aye endureth,
Deep his wisdom, passing thought:
Splendour, light and life attend him,
Beauty springeth out of naught.
Evermore, from his store,
Newborn worlds rise and adore.

Daily doth th'almighty Giver
Bounteous gifts on us bestow;
His desire our soul delighteth;
Pleasure leads us where we go.
Love doth stand at his hand;
Joy doth wait on his command.

Still from man to God eternal
Sacrifice of praise be done,
High above all praises praising
For the gift of Christ, his Son.
Christ doth call one and all:
Ye who follow shall not fall.

All my hope on God is founded

All my hope on God is founded was translated from the German of Joachim Neander by Robert Bridges, later to become Poet Laureate, and appeared in English in 1899 in the *Yattendon Hymnal*. It was a time of transition in Britain; the Great Century was ending, Queen Victoria's life was drawing to its close and many old certainties were no longer quite as certain. The British Empire seemed to be still at its peak, though to those with eyes to see the cracks were appearing. Only two years before, the Queen's Diamond Jubilee had been celebrated with magnificent pomp and circumstance; then came the Boer wars, waged by a handful of farmers who defied the greatest empire the world has ever seen.

Robert Bridges caught that mood in this hymn. It is a dignified, powerful call for Christians to remember that God is God, and to distrust all earthly power. His own background was privileged and he had every reason to be confident in the righteousness of the British ruling class. But he writes:

> *Pride of man and earthly glory,*
> *Sword and crown betray his trust;*
> *What with care and toil he buildeth,*
> *Tower and temple fall to dust.*

There is perhaps a deliberate echo of Kipling's poem *Recessional*, composed for the Jubilee in 1897:

> *Far-called, our navies melt away;*
> *On dune and headland sinks the fire:*
> *Lo, all our pomp of yesterday*
> *Is one with Nineveh and Tyre!*
> *Judge of the Nations, spare us yet,*
> *Lest we forget – lest we forget!*

He also refers to 'lesser breeds without the Law' – the Germans whose imperialistic ambitions were already threatening the peace of the world.

The original writer, Joachim Neander, was only 30 when he died in 1680, probably of tuberculosis. He was born just after the Thirty Years War, which had depopulated and ruined the region we now call Germany, and knew all too well what 'pride of man and earthly glory' could do; the stability which followed was a far better testament to the loving purposes of God. There is a note of thanksgiving in the second half of the hymn which perhaps reflects this greater sense of security:

Daily doth th'almighty Giver
Bounteous gifts on us bestow;
His desire our soul delighteth,
Pleasure leads us where we go.

In spite of its old-fashioned language, this is a very modern hymn. It rebukes the false national pride which leads to military adventurism and calls us to trust in God, who guides us through change and chance.

Neander was a deeply respected pastor and poet, after whom the Neanderthal, near Dusseldorf, is named. He was also a musician and composed *Meine Hoffnung*, to which *All my hope* is usually sung, though the livelier *Michael* by Herbert Howells is also popular; this tune is named after the composer's son, who was born in 1925 and died of meningitis in 1935.

*All things bright and beautiful,
All creatures great and small,
All things wise and wonderful:
The Lord God made them all.*

*Each little flower that opens,
Each little bird that sings,
God made their glowing colors,
He made their tiny wings.*

*The purple-headed mountains,
The river running by,
The sunset and the morning
That brightens up the sky.*

*The cold wind in the winter,
The pleasant summer sun,
The ripe fruits in the garden:
God made them every one.*

*He gave us eyes to see them,
And lips that we might tell
How great is God Almighty,
Who has made all things well.*

All things bright and beautiful

IT is a favourite at weddings, if only because it is one of the few hymns most couples remember from their school assemblies. But *All things bright and beautiful*, when it is sung well, is a delightful and sprightly tour of the created world, offering it in praise to its creator.

It was written by the Irish hymn-writer Mrs Cecil Frances Alexander (1818-1895), wife of a Church of Ireland clergyman who became Bishop of Derry and Archbishop of Armagh, and published in *Hymns for Little Children* in 1848. She was strongly influenced by the Oxford Movement, which sought to restore the Anglican High Church tradition, and particularly by its founder John Keble. Himself a prolific hymn-writer, he encouraged her and edited one of her anthologies.

At one level, it is just a straightforward hymn encouraging children to see the world around them as the work of God, and to be grateful for its life and beauty. But there are other layers to it as well.

For instance, it is sometimes described as an anti-evolution hymn. Mrs Alexander, it is said, wrote the hymn as a piece of propaganda attacking the new-fangled theories of Charles Darwin. It is not surprising that it was taken up by Victorian creationists, but it is unlikely that it was written with this in mind given its date. Darwin did not publish *On the Origin of Species* until 1859, well after *All things bright and beautiful* was written. Having said that, John Keble, her mentor, was firmly in the creationist camp. He once spent a coach journey in a furious argument with William Buckland, the geologist, who had begun to show that the world was millions of years old, with Keble claiming that God had planted fossils in the ground to test the faith of scientists.

There is one verse which is usually omitted in modern hymn-books:

> *The rich man in his castle,*
> *The poor man at his gate;*
> *God made them, high or lowly,*
> *And ordered their estate.*

Nowadays the idea that we should all know our place and defer to our betters grates on us. But many Oxford Movement leaders, including Keble, were politically conservative as well as theologically (though Gladstone, a High Church Anglican, was a Liberal). That was the sort of thing which was taught in their pulpits Sunday by Sunday. Indeed it was a sermon preached against people who sought to better their station in life which turned the young Thomas Hardy against church for good.

Another layer of meaning comes from where the hymn was written. Mrs Alexander was rooted in Protestant Ireland, and a stalwart defender of the establishment. The 'rich man in his castle' was an English Protestant; the 'poor man at his gate' was an Irish peasant. The Irish potato famine killed a million people in Ireland between 1845 and 1852, and caused another million to emigrate – and *All things bright and beautiful* was written in 1848.

More straightforwardly, the hymn also echoes the work of William Paley, whose book *Natural Theology* was a standard theological text in the 19th century. He argued that the world showed evidence of having been designed and that therefore there must have been a designer, in the same way that if we found a watch, we would infer the existence of a watchmaker. 'Look around you!' says the hymn; 'It's a beautiful world, and God made it all, so praise him.'

Mrs Alexander was deeply involved in charitable work, with money from her books helping to support the Derry and Raphoe Diocesan Institution for the Deaf and Dumb, which was founded in 1846. The profits from *Hymns for Little Children* were donated to this school.

It is usually sung either to *Bright and Beautiful* by W H Monk, or to Royal Oak, an old dance tune recorded in 1686. That tune is also known as *The 29th of May*, as it is the setting for a song celebrating the Restoration of Charles II in 1660.

The United Church of Canada includes a fourth verse in its hymn book: 'The rocky mountain splendour,/ The lone wolf's haunting call,/ The great lakes and the prairies,/ The forest in the fall ...'

A nd are we yet alive,
And see each other's face?
Glory and thanks to Jesus give
For his almighty grace!

Preserved by power divine
To full salvation here,
Again in Jesus? praise we join
And in his sight appear.

What troubles have we seen,
What mighty conflicts past,
Fightings without, and fears within,
Since we assembled last!

Yet out of all the Lord
Hath brought us by his love;
And still he doth his help afford,
And hides our life above.

Then let us make our boast
Of his redeeming power,
Which saves us to the uttermost,
Till we can sin no more.

Let us take up the cross
Till we the crown obtain,
And gladly reckon all things loss
So we may Jesus gain.

And are we yet alive?

THIS is a fine old Methodist hymn which is traditionally sung on great occasions such as the opening of the Methodist Conference. It has sunk deep into the denomination's soul – no-one would have had the nerve to suggest that it should be omitted from *Singing the Faith*, the latest Methodist hymn book – but it would be a pity if only Methodists sang it.

Charles Wesley himself, the author, lived and died a loyal member of the Church of England and his greatest hymns transcend all boundaries. This, if we are honest, is not one of them. However, it is still worth reading and singing more than 250 years after it was first printed in Wesley's *Hymns and Sacred Poems* (1749).

It is a hymn of fellowship, expressing the deep love of Christian for Christian and the tie that binds more strongly than any human attachment. More than this, though, it expresses a profound sense of our dependence on the power of God for every breath we take. The opening line is quaint, to say the least – after all, there is only one answer to the question 'And are we yet alive', since we are singing it – but Wesley's idea unfolds as the hymn progresses. Life in the 18th century was precarious and often short, so he was more conscious than we are of dependence on God for life and health. All the more reason for us to hear his words today. There is a sense of gratitude that God's people have been spared to meet again:

> *What troubles have we seen,*
> *What mighty conflicts past,*
> *Fightings without, and fears within,*
> *Since we assembled last!*

> *But God has preserved and protected them:*
> *Yet out of all the Lord*
> *Hath brought us by his love;*
> *And still he doth his help afford,*
> *And hides our life above.*

It concludes:

> *Let us take up the cross*
> *Till we the crown obtain,*
> *And gladly reckon all things loss*
> *So we may Jesus gain.*

It cannot really be said that this is one of Charles' great hymns. It does not soar to any poetic heights, and its use of language is pedestrian and plodding. But it does express something that perhaps we need to recover. We tend to take it for granted that one day follows another and that we will be there to see it. We are used to life being orderly and controllable, and tend to feel that we are the ones who control it. But Charles Wesley had a much deeper sense of God's intimate involvement in the life of the world. It was much more biblical, too: the opening chapter of Genesis is all about how God creates a small bubble of habitable space within a chaotic wilderness and sustains it by his Word: our lives are precarious, but safe because we are held in God's hands.

*And can it be that I should gain
An interest in the Saviour's blood?
Died he for me, who caused his pain—
For me, who him to death pursued?
Amazing love! How can it be,
That thou, my God, shouldst die for me?*

*'Tis mystery all: th'Immortal dies:
Who can explore his strange design?
In vain the firstborn seraph tries
To sound the depths of love divine.
'Tis mercy all! Let earth adore,
Let angel minds inquire no more.*

*He left his Father's throne above
So free, so infinite his grace—
Emptied himself of all but love,
And bled for Adam's helpless race:
'Tis mercy all, immense and free,
For O my God, it found out me!*

*Long my imprisoned spirit lay,
Fast bound in sin and nature's night;
Thine eye diffused a quickening ray—
I woke, the dungeon flamed with light;
My chains fell off, my heart was free,
I rose, went forth, and followed thee.*

*No condemnation now I dread;
Jesus, and all in him, is mine;
Alive in him, my living head,
And clothed in righteousness divine,
Bold I approach th'eternal throne,
And claim the crown, through Christ my own.*

And can it be

CHARLES Wesley was by some distance the greatest of English hymn-writers. When we think of his distance from us in time, this is no small achievement. The 18th century's ways of thinking and believing were different from ours, and the fact that his hymns still speak so powerfully to us after 250 years is a tribute to the skill, the passion and the spiritual insight of their composer.

As well as their merits as verse, the strength of Wesley's hymns lies in the directness of their relation to scripture. He read the Bible closely, thought about it deeply and his hymns were the fruit of learning and prayer. The best of them will speak to us as long as the Bible speaks to us.

This is one of them. It begins with an expression of wonder: 'And can it be ...?' In the second verse, the lines 'In vain the first-born seraph tries/ To sound the depths of love divine' are a reference to 1 Peter 1. 12, which speaks of 'the things that have now been announced to you through those who preached the good news to you by the Holy Spirit sent from heaven, things into which angels long to look'.

The third verse which speaks of Jesus having 'emptied himself of all but love' is a reference to Philippians 2. 5-12, in which he 'made himself nothing, taking the form of a servant, being born in the likeness of men' (verse 7).

In the fourth verse we visit Acts. In chapter 12 there is the story of Peter's miraculous escape from prison: 'And behold, an angel of the Lord stood next to him, and a light shone in the cell. He struck Peter on the side and woke him, saying, "Get up quickly." And the chains fell off his hands. And the angel said to him, "Dress yourself and put on your sandals." And he did so. And he said to him, "Wrap your cloak around you and follow me." And he went out and followed him' (7-9).

The fifth of the verses we usually sing moves to Romans 8. Wesley has the whole chapter in mind, but when he writes: 'No condemnation now I dread' he has in mind verse 33 and 34: 'Who shall bring any charge against God's elect? It is God who justifies. Who is to condemn? Christ Jesus is the one who died—more than that, who was raised—who is at the right hand of God, who indeed is interceding for us.'

Samuel Goldwyn, the film-maker, famously said that a film should 'start with an earthquake and build to a climax'. This hymn is rather like that; at least, the thrilling lines:

> *My chains fell off, my heart was free,*
> *I rose, went forth, and followed thee,*

which we might expect to end the hymn, are followed by an even more passionate declaration of faith.

In Charles Wesley's view, human beings are in chains until Christ frees them. The release of Peter from prison stands for his liberating work in the life of every believer. In Acts 12 it is an angel who visits the prison. For Wesley, it is Christ himself: 'I rose, went forth, and followed thee.' The 'quickening' ray from Jesus' eye is literally 'enlivening'; we were dead in trespasses and sins, but Jesus has raised us to life.

There is a verse which is rightly no longer generally sung, but which is still interesting in what it tells us about Charles Wesley's thinking. The original penultimate verse is this:

> *Still the small inward voice I hear,*
> *That whispers all my sins forgiven;*
> *Still the atoning blood is near,*
> *That quenched the wrath of hostile heaven.*
> *I feel the life his wounds impart;*
> *I feel the Saviour in my heart.*

Sung before the final 'No condemnation' verse it makes perfect sense and fits the Wesleyan belief in the inner witness of Christ's spirit, the felt experience of grace which was the assurance of salvation. We are rightly uneasy with the idea that the blood of Christ 'quenched the wrath of hostile heaven', though; it promotes the idea that Jesus and his Father were somehow on opposing sides in the drama of salvation, which is not the case.

Its marvellous tune, *Sagina*, is by Thomas Campbell (1800-1876); it appeared in a book of hymn tunes entitled *Bouquet*, published in 1825. Nothing else is known of him.

*At even, ere the sun was set,
The sick, O Lord, around thee lay;
O, with what divers pains they met!
O, with what joy they went away!*

*Once more 'tis eventide, and we,
Oppressed with various ills, draw near;
What if thyself we cannot see?
We feel and know that thou art near.*

*O Saviour Christ, our woes dispel;
For some are sick, and some are sad;
And some have never loved thee well,
And some have lost the love they had.*

*And some are pressed with worldly care
And some are tried with sinful doubt;
And some such grievous passions tear,
That only thou canst cast them out.*

*And some have found the world is vain,
Yet from the world they break not free;
And some have friends who give them pain,
Yet have not sought a friend in thee.*

*And none, O Lord, have perfect rest,
For none are wholly free from sin;
And they who long to serve thee best
Are conscious most of wrong within.*

*O Saviour Christ, thou too art man;
Thou hast been troubled, tempted, tried;
Thy kind but searching glance can scan
The very wounds that shame would hide.*

*Thy touch has still its ancient power.
No word from thee can fruitless fall;
Hear, in this solemn evening hour,
And in thy mercy heal us all.*

At even, ere the sun was set

THE story goes that this hymn was composed in a classroom at Godolphin School in Hammersmith in 1868. Henry Twells was the headmaster, and had to wait for a student to finish an examination. It was late afternoon, and the words of Matthew 8. 16-17 came to him and formed the first line of the hymn.

The gospel story itself is very moving, because it is told so simply. 'When evening came, many who were demon-possessed were brought to him, and he drove out the spirits with a word and healed all the sick.' There is no drama, just a statement of fact.

For Henry Twells, the spiritual and physical oppression and sickness overcome by Jesus are translated into our own experience. He tells our story just as simply, but with great wisdom. An Anglican clergyman influenced by the Oxford Movement, the High Church revival of the 19th century, he was steeped in the old spiritual disciplines of the Church of England. Self-examination and holy living were the keynotes of his spirituality, and these are expressed in the hymn.

> *O Saviour Christ, our woes dispel:*
> *For some are sick, and some are sad,*
> *And some have never loved thee well,*
> *And some have lost the love they had.*

None, he says, have perfect rest; none are wholly free from sin, and 'they who long to serve you best/ Are conscious most of wrong within'. He is writing out of his own experience, as a curate in Berkhamstead and as a head teacher; one way or another, there was probably very little that he had not seen.

The verses move effortlessly to Christ himself, who has 'been troubled, tempted, tried'. Because he is human, he can sympathise with our weaknesses, and judge us kindly for our sins.

One of the strengths of the hymn is its simple but powerful use of language. It avoids over-blown rhetoric. It is not grand or showy; it is just a meditation on what goes wrong in our lives, and how Jesus can put it right. It flows so naturally that we could almost feel it is a spontaneous prayer, rather than the highly-skilled piece of verse it actually is.

The last stanza is particularly beautiful, including the whole congregation – many of whom, in a respectable Victorian church, might well feel that they did not particularly need forgiving.

Thy touch still hath its ancient power,
No word from thee can fruitless fall;
Hear in this solemn evening hour,
And in thy mercy heal us all.

Henry Twells died in 1900 in Bournemouth at the age of 76. He was involved in two churches there, St Stephen's and St Augustine's, both of them exceptionally beautiful buildings well worth a visit.

The hymn is usually sung to *Angelus,* by Georg Joseph (1630-1668), a Prussian court musician.

*Blest be the tie that binds
Our hearts in Christian love;
The fellowship of kindred minds
Is like to that above.*

*Before our Father's throne
We pour our ardent prayers;
Our fears, our hopes, our aims are one
Our comforts and our cares.*

*We share each other's woes,
Our mutual burdens bear;
And often for each other flows
The sympathizing tear.*

*When for a while we part
This thought shall ease our pain:
That we shall still be joined in heart,
And hope to meet again.*

*This glorious hope revives
Our courage by the way;
While each in expectation lives,
And longs to see the day.*

*From sorrow, toil and pain,
And sin, we shall be free,
And perfect love and friendship reign
Through all eternity.*

Blest be the tie that binds

SOME hymns have crossed all denominational boundaries while retaining a special place in the affections of Christians belonging to a particular tradition. Many of Charles Wesley's great Methodist hymns have travelled like this, but *Blest be the tie that binds* is a Baptist offering.

The story is that its author, the talented Dr John Fawcett (1740-1817), when he was pastor of the Baptist chapel at Wainsgate in Yorkshire, was called to a larger and more influential church in London. Having preached his farewell sermon, the wagon was loaded with all his books and furniture and he and his wife were ready to go.

His congregation, distraught at the thought of losing him, gathered round them and begged him to stay. His wife said, 'Oh John, John, I cannot bear this.'

'Neither can I, and we will not go,' he replied. 'Unload the wagons and put everything as it was before.'

The first verse of the hymn is quite appropriate to the occasion, and the first three verses are moving reflections on the emotional and spiritual bonds which Christians share. Belonging to a church involves a commitment to vulnerability, and it is costly.

> *We share our mutual woes,*
> *Our mutual burdens bear,*
> *And often for each other flows*
> *The sympathising tear.*

Easier by far to walk away and not form the deep relationships which are so painful when death or sickness comes.

Churches also provide one of the few spaces now where friendships are formed across the generations, and a younger person could expect to face the loss of an older friend. But it is these committed relationships which bring wisdom and shape Christian character, as John Fawcett knew very well.

He did eventually leave Wainsgate, but had a long and fruitful ministry there. Perhaps he knew that he would when he wrote the hymn; the fourth verse speaks of parting – death, perhaps, or simply moving on. In any case, it looks forward to the time when all shall be well – when:

> *From sorrow, toil and pain,*
> *And sin, we shall be free*
> *And perfect love and friendship reign*
> *Through all eternity.*

It has been uncharitably suggested that the Wainsgate congregation might have lived to regret pressing the Fawcetts to stay! Very few pastorates last an entire ministry, and it is usually best for minister and people if he or she can be presented with fresh challenges in new contexts. But there is a right time in God's scheme of things for this to happen, and perhaps, for John Fawcett and Wainsgate, the time was not then.

Is is great verse? No, not really; it is rather clunky, and it does not have the imaginative wings of the best of Charles Wesley. The usual tune does it no favours, to modern ears, either; it is sung generally to Dennis, by the Swiss composer Hans Nägeli (1773-1836), which has dated. However, it expresses deep truths simply and powerfully and it should still be remembered and sung.

In my own first pastorate, I would pray with an elderly couple after each visit, and we would always say the first verse together in closing, as a sort of benediction. When Graham died, I would say it with Mary; but Graham was included too. Now Mary too has died, but when I sing it today I still sing it with them: the same tie binds believers, whether on earth or in heaven.

Break thou the bread of life,
Dear Lord, to me,
As thou didst break the loaves
Beside the sea;
Beyond the sacred page
I seek thee, Lord;
My spirit pants for thee, O living Word!

Bless thou the truth, dear Lord,
To me, to me,
As thou didst bless the bread
By Galilee;
Then shall all bondage cease,
All fetters fall;
And I shall find my peace,
My all in all.

Thou art the bread of life,
O Lord, to me,
Thy holy Word the truth
That saveth me;
Give me to eat and live
With thee above;
Teach me to love thy truth,
For thou art love.

O send thy Spirit, Lord,
Now unto me,
That he may touch my eyes,
And make me see:
Show me the truth concealed
Within thy Word,
And in thy book revealed
I see the Lord.

Break thou the bread of life

THIS is a very rich devotional hymn which takes a theme which is surprisingly unusual, particularly for Nonconformists: the scriptures. The historic Dissenting churches like the Baptists and Congregationalists, the Wesleyans and the newer evangelical churches all, to various degrees, claim to take the authority for their doctrine and practice from the Bible rather than from a heirarchy or from a particular tradition. But there are very few hymns which focus specifically on the Bible; on the face of it, a strange omission.

On the other hand, different interpretations of the Bible have often been deeply divisive. Particular doctrines have been fought over in pulpits and lecture halls; differences regarding the fundamental principles of how to read it have led to mutual excommunications and denominational fragmentations. It is 'inspired', God-breathed – every Christian would agree with that – but what exactly that means is a question never likely to be settled to everyone's satisfaction. 'Christians have burnt each other, quite persuaded/ That all the Apostles would have done as they did', wrote Byron: sadly, all too true.

The strength of *Break thou the bread of life* is that it soars above controversy and focuses on the Bible as a source of spiritual nourishment, given by Christ to his followers. It is bread for the journey, bread broken 'as thou didst break the loaves/ Beside the sea'. Nevertheless, the first verse says: 'Beyond the sacred page/ I seek thee, Lord ...' The scriptures point to Christ, they are not an end in themselves.

However, the third verse begins, 'Thou art the bread of life, to me, to me'. There is something of a contradiction here, perhaps explained by the fact that the hymn is by two different authors. Mary Lathbury wrote the first two verses in 1877. The daughter of a Methodist minister in New York, she was a well-known writer in her day. The third and fourth verses are by Alexander Groves (1842-1909), published posthumously in 1913 in the Wesleyan Methodist Magazine. He was a church organist; not much is known about him otherwise.

There are, of course, many biblical references in this hymn about the Bible. The opening verse refers to the feeding of the 5,000, the only miracle that is related in all four gospels. It stands for the superabundance of God's gracious provision for his people. Mary Lathbury takes it as an image of the inexhaustible spiritual riches of the scriptures.

'My spirit pants for thee' is understandably often printed as 'longs for thee'; 'pants' is a little undignified. But the alternative loses the biblical connection with Psalm 42. 1, 'As a deer pants for flowing streams,/ so pants my soul for you, O God,' which is a pity.

The 'living Word' in the first verse is a reference to John 1, where Christ is described as the Word of God, or to 1 Peter 1. 23 which speaks of the 'living and abiding word of God'.

Alexander Groves, too, was soaked in scripture. 'Thou art the bread of life' is an acknowledgement of Jesus' words in John 6. 22, 'I am the bread of life; whoever comes to me shall not hunger, and whoever believes in me shall never thirst.' When he prays in verse 4 that the Spirit may 'touch my eyes/ And make me see' he is referring to Jesus' healing of a blind man by touching his eyes (Mark 8. 22-26).

Break thou the bread of life is a good hymn to sing before the sermon. It is also a good hymn for a preacher to read before she begins to prepare the sermon, or for any Christian to read before opening the scriptures. These are words of gratitude, humility and awe. God makes himself known through words, and these words point to the living Word.

Breathe on me, breath of God,
Fill me with life anew,
That I may love what thou dost love,
And do what thou wouldst do.

Breathe on me, breath of God,
Until my heart is pure,
Until with thee I will one will,
To do and to endure.

Breathe on me, breath of God,
Till I am wholly thine,
Until this earthly part of me
Glows with thy fire divine.

Breathe on me, breath of God,
So shall I never die,
But live with thee the perfect life
Of thine eternity.

Breathe on me, breath of God

THERE is an Old Testament passage which would send chills up the spine if it were not forever associated with a comic song.

But go back to Ezekiel's original, and 'dem dry bones' are anything but comical. In chapter 37 the prophet speaks of being set in a valley full of bones. God asks him, 'Son of Man, can these bones live?' A suitably cautious answer is met by a demonstration of God's power, as – and we cannot avoid the image of the hip-bone connected to the thigh-bone, and so on – 'there was a noise, a rattling sound, and the bones came together, bone to bone. I looked, and tendons and flesh appeared on them and skin covered them ...'

The miracle is complete, however, when the breath of God enters them and they stand on their feet, as a vast army.

The story was undoubtedly in the mind of Edwin Hatch (1835-1889) when he wrote *Breathe on me, breath of God*.

An Anglican priest, Hatch became professor of classics at Trinity College in Toronto and rector of a high school in Quebec before returning to academia in Oxford. He was a considerable scholar, but of all his works this hymn is the one to have survived.

The story in Ezekiel is about the parlous state of the people of Israel in exile. Their national glory is long gone, and they needed a promise of hope for the future. Though they were nothing but dry bones, God would restore them to life again.

The Church in England in the mid-19th century, for all its trials and doctrinal squabbles, was in a far healthier state than it had been 50 years before; the Evangelicals and the Oxford Movement between them had rescued it. So Hatch makes the Pentecost moment of the Spirit into something deeply personal. He cannot say that the nation needs a revival, but he knows enough of the human heart to know that every Christian does.

However, his vision is not of a quiet, inoffensive piety which consists of good works and soft words. It owes more to the great mystics like Teresa of Avila and John of the Cross. He imagines the Christian soul lost in God, transformed in this world into the likeness of Christ by the indwelling of the Spirit of God.

We are rather used to the words, and sing them too easily. A prayer that God will bring us to the point where we love what he loves, will what he wills, 'until this earthly part of me/ Glows with thy fire divine' is not to be made lightly.

Breathe on me, breath of God is one of those hymns which should endure, and be sung, if only because it reminds us that all our social activism and evangelistic zeal will only flourish if they are rooted in personal devotion to Christ.

*By gracious powers so wonderfully sheltered,
and confidently waiting come what may,
we know that God is with us night and morning
and never fails to greet us each new day.*

By gracious powers, so wonderfully sheltered

DIETRICH Bonhoeffer was a German Lutheran pastor and theologian who became part of the anti-Nazi resistance movement. He paid the ultimate price for his involvement in the July Plot to assassinate Hitler; he was hanged on April 9, 1945, at the age of 39. However, his writings have been influential ever since, and he is revered throughout the world for his courage and his theological insights.

He is not well-known as a hymn-writer, but one of his hymns was translated a few years ago and deserves to be more widely used. Rendered into English by Keith Clements and F Pratt Green and sung to *Finlandia*, it is a profound reflection on suffering and Christian faith, which closes on a note of quiet trustfulness. It is also very recognisably in the tradition of the great Reformation hymns by Joachim Neander and others, in its direct reference to the powers of evil and appeal to the power of God as a shield and refuge.

It is easy to see it in a reflection of his own experience. The second verse runs:

*Yet are our hearts by their old foe tormented,
Still evil days bring burdens hard to bear;
O give our frightened souls the sure salvation
For which, O Lord, you taught us to prepare.*

Bonhoeffer tried to rouse the German Church to a sense of the evils of Nazism, with limited success; Catholics were more inclined to resist than Protestants, who were either seduced by Nazi propaganda into a perverted patriotism or had a theologically-based reluctance to engage in political action. They believed that the crucial issue was freedom to worship, and stepped back from confrontation as long as their own liberty was not under threat.

Bonhoeffer's political activity flowed from a very deep faith, which survived all his reverses. The third verse runs:

> *And when the cup you give is full to brimming*
> *With bitter suffering, hard to understand,*
> *We take it gladly, trusting though with trembling,*
> *Out of so good and so beloved a hand.*

His own suffering was played out on a world stage. Our own is much more personal. We face bereavement, illness, redundancy, and family problems; we worry about money and relationships, and things do go wrong sometimes for all of us. But Bonhoeffer's hymn encourages us to see God's hand at work in everything that happens, the bad as well as the good. He does not believe that God deliberately afflicts us for no good reason; he just invites us to continue to trust, in the knowledge that God is love. And, the hymn concludes:

> *If once again, in this mixed world, you give us*
> *The joy we had, the brightness of your sun*
> *We shall recall what we have learned through sorrow*
> *And dedicate our lives to you alone.*

Christ is risen! Hallelujah!
  Risen our victorious head;
Sing his praises; Hallelujah!
Christ is risen from the dead.
Gratefully our hearts adore him,
As his light once more appears;
Bowing down in joy before him,
Rising up from griefs and tears.

> Christ is risen: Hallelujah!
> Risen our victorious head;
> Sing his praises; Hallelujah!
> Christ is risen from the dead.

Christ is risen! All the sadness
Of his earthly life is o'er;
Through the open gates of gladness
He returns to life once more;
Death and hell before him bending,
He doth rise the victor now,
Angels on his steps attending,
Glory round his wounded brow.

Christ is risen! Henceforth never
Death nor hell shall us enthral;
We are Christ's, in him forever
We have triumphed over all;
All the doubting and dejection
Of our trembling hearts have ceased,
'Tis the day of resurrection;
Let us rise and keep the feast.

Christ is risen! Hallelujah!

EASTER hymns are rightly joyful and triumphant in tone, with a tone of rejoicing that might be solemn or rather sprightly. Ones designed for full-throated congregational singing need to have a strong rhythm and a good tune. The ones which last and feed our spirits also have words which are imaginative, confident and theologically clear.

Christ is risen! Hallelujah! ticks all these boxes. It is an Easter favourite for all these reasons, and is sung in every English-language Christian tradition.

There is a subtle thematic progression through its verses. The first deals with our response to the fact of resurrection, the praise, gratitude and joy with which we greet the risen Lord. The second focuses on Christ himself, coming like a conqueror 'through the open gates of gladness' – the gates of Hell seen from the other side!

The third brings the theology home, as the author – a good pastor – draws out the implications of the Resurrection for our lives today. 'Henceforth never/ Death nor hell shall us enthral ... All the doubting and dejection/ Of our trembling hearts have ceased ...'

John Samuel Bewley Monsell (1811-1875) wrote around 300 hymns. A number of them are still sung today, the most famous of them perhaps *Fight the good fight with all thy might, I hunger and I thirst,* and *O worship the Lord in the beauty of holiness.*

He was born and educated in Ireland, the son of the archdeacon of Londonderry, but ministered in Surrey from 1853 until his death. He wrote many books, one of which, *Our New Vicar*, was republished as recently as 2007 (Kessinger Publishing).

No clergyman of the time could be indifferent to the turmoils of the Church of England and the battles between evangelicals and Anglo-Catholics. But *Our New Vicar*, designed as a help to parishioners facing a change of ministry, shows that he had a warm and pastoral heart more concerned that people should be cared for than that one party or another should win.

His personal life had its tragedies, as most people's did in those days. One son, Thomas, died in a shipwreck on the way to the Crimean War in 1855, aged 18; a daughter died aged only 28. Monsell himself died in an accident, struck by masonry which fell from the roof of his church as it was being rebuilt.

The tune to which *Christ is risen!* is sung, *Morgenlied*, is by Frederick Charles Maker of Bristol (1844-1927). He was a prolific composer, a Free Church Organist, visiting Professor of Music at Clifton College, and conducted the famous Bristol Free Church Choir Association which was such a feature of life in the city.

Come down, O love divine,
Seek thou this soul of mine,
And visit it with thine own ardour glowing.
O Comforter, draw near,
Within my heart appear,
And kindle it, thy holy flame bestowing.

O let it freely burn,
Till earthly passions turn
To dust and ashes in its heat consuming;
And let thy glorious light
Shine ever on my sight,
And clothe me round, the while my path illuming.

Let holy charity
Mine outward vesture be,
And lowliness become mine inner clothing;
True lowliness of heart,
Which takes the humbler part,
And o'er its own shortcomings weeps with loathing.

And so the yearning strong,
With which the soul will long,
Shall far outpass the power of human telling;
For none can guess its grace,
Till he become the place
Wherein the Holy Spirit makes his dwelling.

Come down, O love divine

IT USED to be said that Evangelicals believed in the Father, the Son and the Holy Scripture. One of the enduring aspects of the Renewal movement of the 1970s was the rediscovery of the Spirit. Songs were written which were intimate and direct, expressing the simple joy of personal communion with God.

Over the centuries of the Christian faith this is a pattern which has been repeated again and again. When Church heirarchies get too powerful or congregations become too legalistic, the Spirit of God breaks into the experience of ordinary Christians, renewing the Church from below.

One such movement saw this great hymn by Biano da Siena (d.1434). Very little is known about him. He entered a religious order of unordained men who followed the rule of St Augustine, and wrote hymns which in 1851 were collected and published.

Come Down, O Love Divine was translated by Richard Littledale (1833-1890), an Anglican clergyman and High Churchman who wanted to recover for the Church of England the treasures of the Christian spirituality of the past. A very learned man, he wrote or translated many hymn and works of scholarship; this is the best-known of all his works. It represents four of Bianco's eight verses.

It is full of theology. The Spirit is the one who comes to us and changes us, making us into his own temple. We take on his nature, changed to become like him: the hymn calls on the Spirit to 'burn/ Till earthly passions turn/ To dust and ashes in its heat consuming'.

It is also full of feeling, being a deeply personal statement of faith and longing for deeper communion with God. It speaks of 'the yearning strong/ With which the soul shall long'. There is a deep consciousness of sin, because in the light of God all our human imperfections are heightened: so our inmost self 'o'er its own shortcomings weeps with loathing'.

In its complexity and depth of thought this hymn is a world away from the triviality of much that is written about the Spirit today. Bianco – and his interpreter, Littledale – were steeped in prayer, and had read and thought deeply. They knew that they were seeking union with God, and in wonderfully rich poetry they expressed their longing in words which resonate with us today.

Come Down, O Love Divine is usually sung to *Down Ampney*, by Ralph Vaughan Williams. It is a beautiful tune, but he came to dislike it and attempted to have it withdrawn.

Come, let us sing of a wonderful love,
Tender and true,
Out of the heart of the Father above,
Streaming to me and to you:
Wonderful love,
Dwells in the heart of the Father above.

Jesus the Saviour this Gospel to tell
Joyfully came,
Came with the helpless and hopeless to dwell,
Sharing their sorrow and shame:
Seeking the lost,
Saving, redeeming at measureless cost.

Jesus is seeking the wanderers yet;
Why do they roam?
Love only waits to forgive and forget;
Home, weary wanderers, home!
Wonderful love,
Dwells in the heart of the Father above.

Come to my heart, O thou wonderful love!
Come and abide,
Lifting my life till it rises above
Envy and falsehood and pride:
Seeking to be,
Lowly and humble, a learner of thee.

Come, let us sing of a wonderful love

THIS is a hymn which is sometimes written off as a piece of Victorian sentimentality. Lots of Victorian hymns were not very good, certainly, but this is one which quite rightly is still sung today.

It is deeply felt rather than sentimental. It is written out of a full heart, and a profound sense of how much God has done for us.

It is also a hymn soaked in scripture and shows how deeply the stories of Jesus had sunk into the heart of the author, Robert Walmsley.

The first verse, which speaks of the wonderful love 'streaming to me and to you' recalls God's promise to 'open the windows of heaven' and bless his people: 'Prove me now herewith, saith the LORD of hosts, if I will not open you the windows of heaven, and pour you out a blessing, that there shall not be room enough to receive it' (Malachi 3. 10, KJV). The second and third take their line from the parable of the Lost Sheep (Matthew 18. 12): Jesus came 'seeking the lost/ Saving, redeeming at measureless cost'; he is 'seeking the wanderers yet/ Why do they roam?' There are echoes of the parable of the Prodigal Son, too (Luke 15. 11-32) – 'Love only waits to forgive and forget;/ Home, weary wanderers, home!'

The last verse is a plea for the Spirit to come and indwell us, lifting us above envy, and falsehood, and pride. We cannot ask God to bring others without asking him to deal with us, too. Far from being sentimental, this verse echoes the themes of the great mystics, who sought to lose themselves in God.

The hymn is metrically quite complicated, and it is a mark of the author's skill that we do not notice that as we sing. He does not strain after rhymes and each line flows naturally, leading us further into his own experience of the love of God.

Robert Walmsley was born in Manchester in 1831 and worked as a jeweller in nearby Sale, where he died in 1905. He was involved for many years with the Manchester Sunday School Union, and wrote many hymns for the annual Whit-week Festival, when the children would march through the town in procession.

Very few of them are sung now, but judging by what has survived he had considerable gifts as a writer of devotional verse. An evening hymn, *The sun declines*, is particularly beautiful:

> *The sun declines; o'er land and sea*
> *Creeps on the night;*
> *The twinkling stars come one by one*
> *To shed their light;*
> *With thee there is no darkness, Lord;*
> *With us abide,*
> *And 'neath thy wings we rest secure*
> *This eventide.*

Forgive the wrong this day we've done,
Or thought, or said;
Each moment with its good or ill
To thee has fled;
O Father, in thy mercy great
Will we confide;
Thy benediction now bestow
This eventide.

Come, ye thankful people, come,
Raise the song of harvest home;
All is safely gathered in,
Ere the winter storms begin.
God our maker doth provide
For our wants to be supplied;
Come to God's own temple, come,
Raise the song of harvest home.

All the world is God's own field,
Fruit unto his praise to yield;
Wheat and tares together sown
Unto joy or sorrow grown;
First the blade and then the ear,
Then the full corn shall appear;
Lord of harvest, grant that we
Wholesome grain and pure may be.

For the Lord our God shall come,
And shall take his harvest home;
From his field shall in that day
All offences purge away,
Give his angels charge at last
In the fire the tares to cast;
But the fruitful ears to store
In his garner evermore.

Even so, Lord, quickly come,
Bring thy final harvest home;
Gather thou thy people in,
Free from sorrow, free from sin,
There, forever purified,
In thy presence to abide;
Come, with all thine angels, come,
Raise the glorious harvest home.

Come, ye thankful people, come

THIS hymn is part of almost every harvest service in the country. It has become one of our best-known hymns, cheerfully sung in churches and schools up and down the land. However, it is by no means just a cosy celebration of the countryside, as we might imagine it to be.

It was written by an Anglican clergyman, Henry Alford (1810-1871) who had a significant ministry in Leicestershire before moving to London and then becoming Dean of Canterbury Cathedral. He wrote numerous hymns, some of which are still sung today, notably *Ten thousand times ten thousand/ In sparkling raiment bright* and *Forward! be our watchword*.

Come, ye thankful people, come is the best-known of these. It does begin as a hymn of thanksgiving – that 'All is safely gathered in, ere the winter storms begin' was a matter of relief in those days when rural poverty was widespread and a bad harvest meant real hunger.

However, Alford quickly raises his sights. From considering the needs of the body he moves on to the needs of the soul. 'All the world,' says the second verse, 'is God's own field'. He is referring to the parable of Jesus about the wheat and the tares in Matthew 13. 24-30. The farmer sows good seeds, but finds that weeds grow in his field as well. Rather than root them up immediately and risk destroying the wheat, he waits until the harvest.

So in Alford's hymn, the harvest safely gathered in becomes an image of judgement at the end of the age, expressed in solemn, even frightening terms, borrowed from the Old Testament prophecies about the Day of the Lord:

> *For the Lord our God shall come,*
> *And shall take his harvest home;*
> *From his field shall in that day*
> *All offences purge away,*
> *Give his angels charge at last*
> *In the fire the tares to cast ...*

It is a hymn of confidence – God's people will be saved, stored in his 'garner' or barn for ever – but there is a warning that judgement is not just for people, but against them as well.

As poetry, the hymn is competent rather than inspired; Alford knows what he wants to say, and says it clearly. However, it does have two things to say to us. First, it reminds us that earlier generations were less squeamish about preaching and teaching on themes like judgement. We are much less likely to sing about such things today, but they are a major theme in scripture. Perhaps we need to find better ways of dealing with serious themes – and it is worth saying that Henry Alford himself was not at all gloomy in character, but notably gregarious and cheerful.

Second, there is something very natural about the way in which Alford takes a scene from nature and draws a spiritual lesson from it. This is in keeping with his own Christian tradition: he was a high Anglican, and scholars like John Keble (also a hymn writer) had encouraged people to rediscover the teachings of the early Church, whose scholars saw God revealed in his works, as well as his word. In this, of course, they were following the example of Jesus himself, who used ordinary situations and country scenes to teach Gospel truths. If we open our eyes to the world around us and see it with an imaginative spirituality, we will find ourselves enriched by what is around us.

*C*ome, thou fount of every blessing,
Tune my heart to sing thy grace;
Streams of mercy, never ceasing,
Call for songs of loudest praise.
Teach me some melodious measure,
Sung by flaming tongues above.
O the vast, the boundless treasure
Of my Lord's unchanging love.

Here I raise mine Ebenezer;
Hither by thy help I'm come;
And I hope, by thy good pleasure,
Safely to arrive at home.
Jesus sought me when a stranger,
Wandering from the fold of God;
He, to rescue me from danger,
Interposed his precious blood.

O to grace how great a debtor
Daily I'm constrained to be!
Let that grace, Lord, like a fetter,
Bind my wandering heart to thee.
Prone to wander, Lord, I feel it,
Prone to leave the God I love;
Take my heart, O take and seal it,
Seal it from thy courts above.

Come, thou fount of every blessing

Come, thou fount of every blessing is a fine hymn that is in danger of passing out of use in the denomination of its writer. It is doubtful whether many Baptists sing it now, or remember its author's story, though it is good to see it in the new Methodist hymn book, *Singing The Faith* and it is in *Combined Mission Praise*.

Robert Robinson (1735-1790) had a bad start in life. His father, a Norfolk customs officer, had married above him and when he died when

Robert was only five, his maternal grandfather disinherited him. He was sent to school by the charity of an uncle, but fell into bad company. However, it was this that was to result in his conversion: tormenting a poor gypsy by making her drunk, he and his friends demanded she tell their fortunes. Pointing at Robert, she told him he would live to see his children and grandchildren. Struck by her words, he decided to change his way of life and went to hear the Methodist preacher George Whitefield, under whose ministry he repented. He wrote his great hymn two years later.

He did not stay long a Methodist, becoming first a Congregationalist and then a Baptist at the Stone-Yard Baptist Chapel in Cambridge, where he remained the rest of his life. A new chapel was built for him in 1764 where his preaching drew crowds of up to 1,000.

Come, thou fount of every blessing is one of the great Nonconformist hymns. It is a profound meditation on grace, soaked in biblical imagery which is less familiar to us than it ought to be. Robinson writes of 'the vast, the boundless treasure/ Of my Lord's unfailing love'. In a memorable line he says: 'Here I raise my Ebenezer' – a reference to the memorial 'stone of help raised by the prophet in 1 Samuel 7. 12, sadly reduced in *Singing The Faith* to 'Here I find my greatest treasure'. The change makes it more singable today, but a layer of meaning is lost. He means to say that his experience of grace and forgiveness is his spiritual lodestone, the reference point around which all his future life will be lived.

The hymn continues:
> *Prone to wander, Lord, I feel it;*
> *Prone to leave the God I love;*
> *Take my heart, O take and seal it*
> *Seal it from thy courts above!*

He may have wandered. It was said – by Unitarians – that towards the end of his life he embraced Unitarianism, though he always denied it. An oft-told story, which may or not be true, is that he was riding in a coach with a lady who asked him what he thought of the hymn she was humming. He is said to have responded: 'Madam, I am the poor unhappy man who wrote that hymn many years ago, and I would give a thousand worlds, if I had them, to enjoy the feelings I had then.'

Feelings do change, and it is unwise to expect them to remain the same. Robert Robinson's hymn, though, speaks of the grace of the unchanging God, and whatever his own experiences, that remains eternal truth.

*Creator Spirit, by whose aid
The world's foundations first were laid:
Come visit every waiting mind,
And pour thy joys on human kind;
From sin and sorrow set us free,
And make us temples worthy thee.*

*Thou source of uncreated light,
The Father's promised Paraclete,
Thrice holy Fount, thrice holy Fire,
Our hearts with heavenly love inspire;
Come, and thy sacred unction bring
To sanctify us while we sing.*

*Plenteous of grace, descend from high,
Rich in thy sevenfold energy;
Thou strength of his almighty hand
Whose power does heaven and earth command,
Refine and purge our earthly parts,
And stamp thine image on our hearts.*

*Immortal honour, endless fame,
Attend the Almighty Father's name;
The Saviour Son be glorified,
Who for lost man's redemption died;
And equal adoration be,
Eternal Paraclete, to thee.*

Creator Spirit, by whose aid

PENTECOST is the birthday of the Church, when the Holy Spirit came on the Apostles and filled them with power and with joy. From being a philosophy of life, Christianity became a living faith. Disciples of Jesus would know the presence of God with them as a source of strength and hope. They would not only be told how to live, but they would be given the resources they needed to choose right.

In years gone by, when Sunday schools were numbered in their hundreds, many churches had Whitsun parades or Whit Walks, when their children would march through the streets under their banners.

In one parade in Manchester in 1930, for instance, no fewer than 20,000 marched. Film footage survives showing the girls dressed in white and carrying flowers.

While those days might be gone, they did say something about how important Pentecost is. Some of the Church's hymns put this into words, and help to mark this as one of the great Christian festivals.

One of them is *Creator Spirit*, by John Dryden (1631-1700). It is from a Latin original, probably written in the 9th century, though its authorship is disputed – candidates include Charlemagne, Ambrose of Milan, Gregory I, and a German monk, Rhabanus Maurus. Dryden translated and improved it.

The hymn is full of theology, and echoes the Bible in every verse. Genesis 1 is recalled in the first, where 'the spirit of God moved upon the face of the waters' – Dryden calls on the Spirit 'by whose aid/ The world's foundations first were laid'. The Spirit is to 'pour thy joys on human kind', and set us free from sin and sorrow. We are his 'temples' – echoes of Paul's words to the Corinthians (I Corinthians 3. 16, 6. 19).

Dryden – the most influential literary figure of the 17th century, a prolific poet, playwright and critic – is able to use words that today we need explained for us. The Spirit is 'The Father's promised Paraclete': the word is Greek, and it means 'one called alongside to help'. It is a description not just of the nature but the ministry of the Spirit, who 'helps us in our weaknesses' (Romans 8. 26). He writes, 'Come, and thy sacred unction bring/ To sanctify us while we sing'. Unction is anointing oil, used in rituals to symbolise that something is purified and made fit for its holy purpose. For Christians, the Spirit's work is all the purification needed.

The last verse is a masterclass in theological subtlety combined with poetic force:

> *Immortal honour, endless fame,*
> *Attend th'almighty Father's name:*
> *The Saviour Son be glorified,*
> *Who for lost man's redemption died:*
> *And equal adoration be,*
> *Eternal Paraclete, to thee.*

The almighty Father has precedence, and then the redeeming Son, but there is no sense that the one is superior to the other. The Spirit, the eternal Paraclete, deserves equal adoration. This is thoroughly Trinitarian verse, in which the Spirit is worshipped as co-equal with the first and second persons. It is a wonderful teaching hymn, still sung in most churches at Pentecost.

Dear Lord and Father of mankind,
Forgive our foolish ways!
Reclothe us in our rightful mind,
In purer lives thy service find,
In deeper reverence, praise.

In simple trust like theirs who heard,
Beside the Syrian sea,
The gracious calling of the Lord,
Let us, like them, without a word,
Rise up and follow thee.

O Sabbath rest by Galilee!
O calm of hills above,
Where Jesus knelt to share with thee
The silence of eternity
Interpreted by love!

Drop thy still dews of quietness
Till all our strivings cease:
Take from our souls the strain and stress,
And let our ordered lives confess
The beauty of thy peace.

Breathe through the heats of our desire
Thy coolness and thy balm;
Let sense be dumb, let flesh retire;
Speak through the earthquake, wind, and fire,
O still, small voice of calm.

Dear Lord and Father of mankind

THIS is a very beautiful devotional hymn by the Quaker poet John Greenleaf Whittier (1807-1892).

As well as being a popular poet and hymn-writer, Whittier was a passionate anti-slavery activist, at a time when feelings ran high enough on both sides to precipitate the American Civil War. Whittier himself was burned out of his office in the anti-slavery centre in Philadelphia in 1838.

Some of his poems and hymns survive. Of these, *Dear Lord and Father* is the most popular. It has a deceptive straightforwardness about it. It argues for simplicity, quietness, calm; perhaps especially in our busy and noisy world, it speaks powerfully of the need to be still and know that God is God.

That was Whittier's intention, but it is not quite as simple as that. *Dear Lord* was not originally a hymn, but part of a longer poem, *The Brewing of Soma* – soma being a hallucinogenic drug used in ancient times to create a counterfeit spiritual experience. According to Whittier,

> *As in the child-world's early year,*
> *Each after age has striven*
> *By music, incense, vigils drear,*
> *And trance, to bring the skies more near,*
> *Or lift men up to heaven!*

In other words, we are still spiritually cheating; instead of listening to the still, small voice of calm,

> *In sensual transports wild as vain*
> *We brew in many a Christian fane (temple)*
> *The heathen Soma still!*

The hymn still speaks to us, and perhaps more clearly when we understand what the poet was really getting at. The Quaker tradition is to come before God in silence, and only to speak when there is something worth saying. Nowadays that is rare; we feel uncomfortable without music, and silence in worship is often awkward. Whittier says that that is not the way to bring God closer to us, or us to God. There is no need to create a mood, either with soft chords and gentle strumming or with loud praise music; that is like drinking soma, and we are still cheating.

So in a way, it is ironic that we sing *Dear Lord and Father* at all. In fact, it does lend itself to prayerful meditation as well as congregational singing, perhaps with different people reading each verse and allowing space for quiet meditation in between.

When it is sung, it is usually to the tune *Repton*, by Hubert Parry. He wrote it in 1888 for his oratorio *Judith*, where it is the setting of a contralto aria, *Long since in Egypt's pleasant land*.

Eternal Father, strong to save,
Whose arm hath bound the restless wave,
Who bid'st the mighty ocean deep
Its own appointed limits keep;
Oh, hear us when we cry to thee,
For those in peril on the sea!

O Christ! Whose voice the waters heard
And hushed their raging at thy word,
Who walkedst on the foaming deep,
And calm amidst the storm didst sleep;
Oh, hear us when we cry to thee,
For those in peril on the sea!

O Holy Spirit! Who didst brood
Upon the chaos dark and rude,
And bid its angry tumult cease,
And give, for wild confusion, peace;
Oh, hear us when we cry to thee,
For those in peril on the sea!

O Trinity of love and power!
Our brethren shield in danger's hour;
From rock and tempest, fire and foe,
Protect them wheresoe'er they go;
And evermore shall rise to thee
Glad hymns of praise from land and sea.

Eternal Father, strong to save

THERE is one hymn which has been inextricably linked to the seafaring tradition of our island nation for 150 years.

Eternal Father, strong to save was written by the Anglican clergyman William Whiting (1825–1878) in 1860. He was the Master of Winchester College Choristers' School, and wrote it for a student who was about to sail for America. Since then it has become known and loved all over the English-speaking world. It speaks powerfully to Royal and Merchant Navy congregations, churches in fishing and cargo ports, and everywhere that folk make their living from the sea – beautiful as it is, but dangerous and unpredictable.

The hymn has a Trinitarian structure, and it is soaked in biblical imagery. Each verse takes an aspect of the world of one of the Persons of the Godhead, and links it to the real experience of God's people in this life. So the first addresses the Eternal Father, whose command 'bound the restless wave'. It is a reference to Job 38. 8-11, where God is reminding Job of his power over nature: he said to the sea, 'Thus far shall you come, and no farther, and here shall your proud waves be stayed.'

The second is a reference to two stories of the power of Christ over the deep water. In Matthew 8. 23-27 there is the story of Jesus stilling the storm on Lake Galilee – 'He rebuked the wind and the sea, and there was a great calm' – the waters 'hushed their raging at thy word'. In John 6. 16-21 Jesus comes to the disciples across the water, walking on the 'foaming deep'.

The third verse addresses the Spirit, and takes us back to Genesis 1. 2, where the pre-Creation is imagined as a vast waste of water, the 'chaos dark and rude' (crude) over which the Spirit brooded. The 'angry tumult' ceased at the word of God, who spoke and brought light and order through the Spirit's creative power.

The Hebrews were not a seafaring race. In the Bible, the sea stands for what is dangerous, chaotic and treacherous. It is linked to pagan conceptions of their deities, and it is a symbol of the darkness and disorder to which God is opposed. In Revelation 21. 1, John's vision of the new, perfect creation is that 'there was no longer any sea'. But God is stronger even than this powerful evil; he limits it, Christ calms it, the Spirit tames it.

Whiting was a good biblical scholar, and understood this well. So his hymn is not just for seafarers; it is for all of us, because all of us are at sea, voyaging on life's way, buffeted by storms and tempests and hoping for a safe landfall. The last verse sums this up perfectly: it is a prayer to the 'Trinity of love and power' to protect us all 'from rock and tempest, fire and foe' – so in a variation to the refrain, 'And evermore shall rise to Thee/ Glad hymns of praise from land and sea.'

The hymn has attracted other verses over the years, to reflect changing times. Mary Hamilton wrote verses beginning 'Lord, guard and guide the men who fly/ Through the great spaces in the sky' in 1915; the science fiction master Robert Heinlein wrote one in 1947 as part of his short story Ordeal in Space.

The hymn is sung to *Melita*, by JB Dykes. He named it, appropriately, after the island where St Paul was shipwrecked, now known as Malta.

*Father of mercies, in thy Word
What endless glory shines!
Forever be thy name adored
For these celestial lines.*

*Here may the blind and hungry come
And light and food receive;
Here shall the lowliest guest have room
And taste and see and live.*

*Here springs of consolation rise
To cheer the fainting mind,
And thirsting souls receive supplies
And sweet refreshment find.*

*Here the Redeemer's welcome voice
Spreads heavenly peace around,
And life and everlasting joys
Attend the blissful sound.*

*Oh, may these heavenly pages be
My ever dear delight;
And still new beauties may I see
And still increasing light!*

*Divine Instructor, gracious Lord,
Be thou forever near;
Teach me to love thy sacred word
And view my Saviour there.*

Father of mercies, in thy Word

THERE are not too many modern hymns which deal with scripture and focus our attention on the written word of God. Perhaps there never have been, but certainly a recurrent theme among observers of today's Church scene is how far we have strayed from our ancestors' immersion in the Bible, in both public and private devotions. In many services in the evangelical and charismatic tradition the Bible is hardly read aloud at all, and fewer of us read it at home, too – a Bible Society report not long ago revealed that only 16 per cent of us read the Bible every day, and 33 per cent do not read it at all.

Of course reading the Bible every day is no guarantee of spiritual growth, and we all know people who can bring every homegroup discussion to a close with a knock-down proof text. But the testimony of the Church throughout the ages has been that we neglect the treasures of the Bible at our spiritual peril.

Father of mercies is a hymn that is full of reverence for the word of God, arising from a deep and intimate knowledge of it. It deserves to be sung more often in spite of the fact that it is rather dated.

Written by the Baptist hymnwriter Anne Steele (1716-1778), in its full version it speaks of 'riches above what earth can grant,' and describes it as a 'fair tree of knowledge' yielding 'richer fruits than nature shows'.

The Bible is our guide in trouble, and our comfort in distress:

> *Here springs of consolation rise*
> *To cheer the fainting mind,*
> *And thirsty souls receive supplies,*
> *And sweet refreshment find.*

Above all, the scriptures point to Jesus: as Miss Steele says, 'Teach me to love thy sacred word,/ And view my Saviour there.'

The strength of the hymn lies in the depth of the experience behind it. This is not a dry theological exhortation, but the record of someone who has found treasures in the Bible and wants to share them.

Anne Steele's poetry and hymns were set against the background of a life that was full of tragedy. When she was only three years old her mother died; at 19 she suffered a hip injury which made her a life-long invalid. She became engaged to be married, but when she was only 21 her fiancé died. Nevertheless, she maintained a quiet trust and faith in God when others might have despaired, and her devotional writing – hymns, and versified Psalms – became enormously popular. She lived all her life in Broughton, Hants, where her father, a timber merchant, was a lay preacher.

When someone who has lived such a difficult life writes of the 'springs of consolation' to be found in the Bible, and says, 'Here the Redeemer's welcome voice/ Spreads heavenly peace around,' we are bound to listen. The language may be old-fashioned, but Anne reminds us of what we may be losing by not taking the scripture as seriously as she.

*Father, hear the prayer we offer:
Nor for ease that prayer shall be,
But for strength, that we may ever
Live our lives courageously.*

*Not forever in green pastures
Do we ask our way to be,
But the steep and rugged pathway
May we tread rejoicingly.*

*Not forever by still waters
Would we idly, quiet stay;
But would smite the living fountains
From the rocks along our way.*

*Be our strength in hours of weakness,
In our wanderings be our guide;
Through endeavour, failure, danger,
Father, be thou at our side.*

*Let our path be bright or dreary,
Storm or sunshine be our share;
May our souls in hope unweary
Make thy work our ceaseless prayer.*

Father, hear the prayer we offer

PSALM 23 is the best loved of all the Psalms. Its promises of green pastures and quiet waters have brought comfort to millions over the centuries. But they can also be used as excuses for inaction. If we luxuriate in songs of praise, empty prayers and undemanding sermons, and don't hear the challenge to take up our cross and follow Christ, we might persuade ourselves that we're spiritually blessed when really we're just spiritually lazy.

Love Maria Willis (1824-1908) was a Unitarian, and a popular lady of letters in Boston and New York. She wrote *Father, hear the prayer we offer* as a reaction against popular sentimentalism. 'Not for ever in green pastures/ Do we ask our way to be ...' 'Not for ever by still waters/ Would we idly quiet stray ...' The echoes of the Psalm are very specific, and they challenge our passive discipleship. In her closing verse, which is not always sung, she says:

> *Let our path be bright or dreary,*
> *Storm or sunshine be our share;*
> *May our souls, in hope unweary,*
> *Make thy work our ceaseless prayer.*

For her, prayer is work, and we should not try to avoid it by fine-sounding words.

Over the last few years there has been a rediscovery in many churches of the ancient disciplines of silence, meditation and fasting. Retreats are booming, and even good evangelicals might have spiritual directors where once they would have fought shy of such Catholic practices. All this is good, but there is a risk that the pendulum will swing too far the other way, and that Christians will retreat into holy huddles. For Willis, it was important to pray not for ease, but for strength to live courageously, whatever God sends us.

She married Frederick Willis in 1858, and through him became linked to a fascinating literary circle. Frederick had been brought up by his grandparents after the death of his parents. His grandfather, a Baptist minister, had thrown him out because Frederick refused to believe in predestination, and at the age of 14 he was taken in by Mrs Alcott, mother of Anna, Louisa, Lizzie and May Alcott – immortalised as Meg, Jo, Beth, and Amy in the novel *Little Women*, written by Louisa. Mrs Alcott regarded him as her son, and he may have been the inspiration for *Little Women*'s hero Laurie. Through the Alcotts he met such literary figures as Emerson, Thoreau and Nathaniel Hawthorne, among others.

Fill thou my life, O Lord my God,
In every part with praise,
That my whole being may proclaim
Thy being and thy ways.

Not for the lip of praise alone,
Nor e'en the praising heart
I ask, but for a life made up
Of praise in every part!

Praise in the common things of life,
Its goings our and in;
Praise in each duty and deed,
However small and mean.

Fill every part of me with praise;
Let all my being speak
Of thee and of thy love, O Lord,
Poor though I be, and weak.

So shalt thou, Lord, from me, e'en me,
Receive the glory due;
And so shall I begin on earth
The song forever new.

So shall each fear, each fret, each care
Be turned into a song,
And every winding of the way
The echo shall prolong;

So shall no part of day or night
From sacredness be free;
But all my life, in every part
Be fellowship with thee.

Fill thou my life, O Lord my God

THERE has been a rich flowering of songwriting over the last few decades, and the Church has been all the richer for it. But the old hymns still speak, and their formal structure and rhythms allow thoughts to be developed over a few verses rather than just a few repeated lines. Some of them will rightly pass out of use, while others have a few more years left in them yet.

Fill thou my life is one of them. Written by the 'prince of Scottish hymn writers', Horatius Bonar (1808-1889), it is a hymn of consecration. He takes the theme of praise, and invites us to offer every part of our life to God; 'a life made up/of praise in every part'. The hymn continues:

> *Praise in the common things of life,*
> *Its goings out and in;*
> *Praise in each duty and each deed,*
> *However small and mean.*

There is a great truth here. We are very inclined to split off our spiritual lives from our everyday experience. Sundays are for church, and possibly a midweek meeting; and we might be very diligent even in our prayer and Bible reading during the week. But there is still a disconnection between this and what we think of as our 'real' life.

The 'life made up of praise in every part', though, is different. We are not necessarily thinking of God in every minute of every day. But every part of our life is to be given to him; our home, family, work, leisure, are all to be consecrated. When an unbeliever looks at us, he or she should see Christ; 'Let all my being speak/ Of thee and of thy love, O Lord/ Poor though I be and weak.'

These are high ambitions, and the hymn is realistic: we rely on God's Spirit to fill our lives, and even the best of us end our lives only as beginners in holiness. For Horatius Bonar, in this hymn as in his other well-loved works, it is grace, not works, that brings us to heaven in the end.

Bonar was born to a substantial middle-class family; his father was Scotland's Solicitor for Excise. He graduated from Edinburgh University and was ordained in 1838 into the Church of Scotland. He joined the Free Church of Scotland after the Disruption of 1843, when many ministers and congregations broke away in protest against what they saw as state interference in the Church's affairs.

He served his congregations in Kelso and Edinburgh well and faithfully throughout a long life which was nevertheless touched with tragedy: he and his wife lost five of their young children in succession, and his daughter's husband, also a minister, died leaving her with five young children; she came to live with them towards the end of their lives.

He wrote more than 600 hymns, of which several are still sung, including *I heard the voice of Jesus say*, and *Blessing and honour and glory and power,* and many books and pamphlets.

For all the saints who from their labours rest,
   Who thee by faith before the world confessed,
Thy name, O Jesus, be forever blest,
Alleluia! Alleluia!

Thou wast their rock, their fortress, and their might;
Thou, Lord, their captain in the well-fought fight;
Thou, in the darkness drear, their one true light.
Alleluia! Alleluia!

Oh, may thy soldiers, faithful, true and bold,
Fight as the saints who nobly fought of old
And win with them the victor's crown of gold.
Alleluia! Alleluia!

O blest communion, fellowship divine,
We feebly struggle, they in glory shine;
Yet all are one in thee, for all are thine.
Alleluia! Alleluia!

And when the fight is fierce, the warfare long,
Steals on the ear the distant triumph song,
And hearts are brave again, and arms are strong.
Alleluia! Alleluia!

But, lo, there breaks a yet more glorious day;
The saints triumphant rise in bright array;
The King of Glory passes on his way.
Alleluia! Alleluia!

From earth's wide bounds, from ocean's farthest coast,
Through gates of pearl streams in the countless host,
Singing to Father, Son, and Holy Ghost,
Alleluia! Alleluia!

The golden evening brightens in the west;
Soon, soon, to faithful warriors cometh rest.
Sweet is the calm of paradise the blest.
Alleluia! Alleluia!

For all the saints who from their labours rest

DEATH is a universal experience. Everyone will lose someone, and there is no escaping it. It is right to grieve, and most people do.

For Christians, though, there is another story as well. We grieve too, but as the Apostle Paul says, 'not like people who have no hope' (1 Thessalonians 4. 13). So the songs and hymns we sing at a funeral service will have a different ring to them than for those who do not believe, or whose faith has ceased to be a living reality.

William Walsham How (1823-1897) was an Anglican clergyman who worked for much of his life in Shropshire, where he is buried, but who spent his most influential years in London as Bishop of Bedford. He worked in the East End and was very popular among the people there, being known as 'the children's bishop'. He became Bishop of Wakefield in 1888, and died in Ireland when he was on holiday.

His best known hymn is *For all the saints*, and it is very different from the usual sort of hymn that might be sung at a funeral – especially sung to the rousing *Sine Nomine* by Vaughan Williams. This hymn strikes a note of celebration. It is not a dirge, and it does not try to express sorrow for the loss of loved ones. How was deeply aware of the sadness of death: he wrote it before he moved to the East End and faced the grim reality of life in the slums there, but anyone – and any minister – in those days was intimately aware of the shortness of life. Nevertheless, this hymn speaks of death as a triumph, not as a tragedy. Those who have died rest from their labours; they have worked hard for the kingdom of God, guided and supported all the way. They are the 'blest communion, fellowship divine/ We feebly struggle, they in glory shine/ Yet all are one in thee, for all are thine ...'

The dead are not defeated: they are a shining example of heroism and victory. 'And when the fight is fierce, the warfare long/ Steals on the ear the distant triumph song ...'

One of the closing verses of the hymn (there are 10, but not every book includes them all) looks forward to the ultimate victory of Christ: 'The King of Glory passes on his way ...'

There is a tremendous paean of confident praise in the final verse, as How imagines all the dead in Christ from all over the world streaming through the gates of heaven, 'singing to Father, Son and Holy Ghost: Alleluia!'

Everyone will grieve at losing someone they love. But a hymn like this – though it may not speak to our hearts when we are in the depths of sorrow – reminds us of another truth, and speaks to us on a different level. Christ has conquered death, and we share in his victory. Death for the Christian is not a defeat, but a triumphal entry into a glorious future.

The name of the tune, too, has a message for us. *Sine nomine* means 'without a name'. The vast majority of Christians die anonymously; there are just a few heroes of the faith whose memory is known and cherished. This is a hymn of praise for the rest of us.

Glorious things of thee are spoken,
  Zion, city of our God;
He whose word cannot be broken
Formed thee for his own abode;
On the Rock of Ages founded,
What can shake thy sure repose?
With salvation's walls surrounded,
Thou may'st smile at all thy foes.

See! the streams of living waters,
Springing from eternal love,
Well supply thy sons and daughters
And all fear of want remove.
Who can faint, when such a river
Ever flows their thirst to assuage?
Grace which, like the Lord, the Giver,
Never fails from age to age.

Round each habitation hovering,
See the cloud and fire appear
For a glory and a covering,
Showing that the Lord is near.
Thus they march, their pillar leading,
Light by night, and shade by day;
Daily on the manna feeding
Which he gives them when they pray.

Blest inhabitants of Zion,
Washed in the Redeemer's blood!
Jesus, whom their souls rely on,
Makes them kings and priests to God.
'Tis his love his people raises
Over self to reign as kings:
And as priests, his solemn praises
Each for a thank-offering brings.

Saviour, if of Zion's city,
I through grace a member am,
Let the world deride or pity,
I will glory in thy name.

Fading is the worldling's pleasure,
All his boasted pomp and show;
Solid joys and lasting treasure
None but Zion's children know.

Glorious things of thee are spoken

JOHN Newton's life story has been told very often, but it is still deeply moving. Taken to sea by his father at the age of seven, he lived a wild life and had no time for religion. Among his many adventures, he lived as a slave in Africa for 15 months, half-starved.

He was converted at the age of 23 through reading the works of the spiritual writer Thomas a Kempis, but his new-found faith did not lead to an instant change of life. He commanded a slave ship, and it was only later that he became an ardent anti-slavery campaigner.

Having studied theology, he was ordained and became curate of Olney in Buckinghamshire in 1764. He became friends with the poet William Cowper, and wrote his *Olney Hymns*.

The most famous of these is *Amazing grace*. But others are still sung, notably *Glorious things of thee are spoken*. It is a hymn to the Church – a rich meditation on the Bride of Christ, for which he died.

As such, it is an unfamiliar theme in many of our churches. Much modern music is very me-centred, about what Jesus means to me and how I feel about him. There is nothing wrong with that as such, and songs that help us express real emotion and spiritual feeling in the language of our time are to be welcomed. But this speaks of the goodness of God to his Church. The hymn is full of biblical imagery: the church is Zion, the City of God, founded on a rock and a secure fortress. It is supplied with rivers of grace; its people are kings and priests, washed in the blood of the Redeemer.

This joyful celebration of the Church is more striking when we think about the 18th century Church of England of which Newton was a member. It was spiritually at a very low ebb, with many of its priests careerists or practical unbelievers. While there were faithful ministers, a wealthy parish was seen as an acceptable position for a younger son of the gentry and many people did very well for themselves. For Newton, however, the Church was primarily spiritual, not a social club or a way of keeping the masses under control.

He wrote of his *Olney Hymns* that 'they should be Hymns, not Odes, if designed for public worship, and for the use of plain people. Perspicuity, simplicity and ease, should be chiefly attended to; and the imagery and colouring of poetry, if admitted at all, should be indulged very sparingly and with great judgement.' In other words, no flowery language; they should be easily understandable.

Language and fashions in verse do change, and it may be that *Glorious things* does not have many more years of usefulness for us. It is no longer as instantly accessible as Newton would have wanted it to be. But if people are given the chance to understand it and think about its meaning, it can be a rich source of blessing.

It is usually sung to the great tune *Austria*, which gives its words a wonderful lift.

God of grace and God of glory,
On thy people pour thy power.
Crown thine ancient Church's story,
Bring her bud to glorious flower.
Grant us wisdom, grant us courage,
For the facing of this hour,

God of grace and God of glory

GOD of grace and God of glory is sung today as a stirring call to spiritual arms in the face of a world in need.

When the US Baptist minister Harry Emerson Fosdick wrote it in 1930, these needs were even more pressing. The First World War had ended with the short-sighted Treaty of Versailles, Germany had been economically crippled and the Nazis were becoming a force. The Depression was biting the American economy as well, and there were grim signs of worse times to come.

Fosdick (1878-1960) was an influential pastor, preacher and teacher based in New York. He was on the front line in the war between liberal and fundamentalist theologians, taking the liberal side. He saw the Bible as the record of God's unfolding purposes for humankind, rather than as a document dictated from on high and infallible. This was more controversial at the time than it would be now, and he faced censure from the General Assembly of the Presbyterian Church (he served as guest preacher at First Presbyterian Church) for a sermon he preached and published entitled 'Shall the fundamentalists win?' He was defended by John Foster Dulles, who rose to high office under President Eisenhower, but Fosdick resigned to become pastor of a Baptist church again. He was outspoken against the racism and intolerance of US society of the time, and was influential in the growth of Alcoholics Anonymous.

So when Fosdick wrote, 'Lo! the hosts of evil 'round us,/ Scorn thy Christ, assail his ways' he would have had particular examples in mind. Fundamentalists were denying the explanatory power of science, which

Fosdick saw as a God-given undertaking which unfolded the wonders of creation. A racist legal system discriminated terribly against black people; Fosdick intervened in the case of the Scottsboro Boys, nine young black men falsely accused of raping two white women. When he wrote, 'Save us from weak resignation,/ To the evils we deplore' he was aware of the temptation, and determined with God's help to resist it. And when he wrote, 'Cure thy children's warring madness,/ Bend our pride to thy control' he may well have seen far enough to realise that the war-clouds were gathering again. He was an opponent of Nazism, but believed in appeasing Hitler as far as possible; the democracies were responsible for the rise of totalitarianism, he thought, through their foolish and misguided policies.

The hymn is still sung today because the world has not changed as much as it ought to have done. We are still 'rich in things and poor in soul'; we still need wisdom and courage to live the life to which Christ calls us. And with the rise of the 'New Atheism', we are once again confronted with those who 'Scorn thy Christ, assail his ways'.

Great God, we sing thy mighty hand
By which supported still we stand;
The opening year thy mercy shows,
That mercy crowns it 'til its close.

By day, by night, at home, abroad,
Still are we guarded by our God,
By his incessant bounty fed,
By his unerring counsel led.

With grateful hearts the past we own;
The future, all to us unknown,
We to thy guardian care commit,
And peaceful leave before thy feet.

In scenes exalted or depressed,
Thou art our joy, and thou our rest;
Thy goodness all our hopes shall raise,
Adored through all our changing days.

When death shall interrupt our songs
And seal in silence mortal tongues,
In fairer realms, O God, shall we
Thy praises sing eternally.

Great God, we sing thy mighty hand

PHILIP Doddridge (1702-1751) was a Nonconformist clergyman who ministered in Northampton. He was a prolific author, a scholar and an influential preacher and teacher; in those days Nonconformists were not allowed to graduate from the English Universities, and Doddridge worked hard as an educator of young people.

His most famous book, *The Rise and Progress of Religion in the Soul*, was translated into seven languages, and was highly praised a century later by the Baptist preacher C H Spurgeon. It was this book that led William Wilberforce, the anti-slave trade campaigner, to become a Christian.

Doddridge wrote more than 400 hymns, most of them based on his sermons and designed to sum up his messages in ways the congregation could understand and remember. A very popular one still sung today is *O God of Bethel, by whose hand.*

Great God, we sing thy mighty hand is very often sung at the beginning of a new year or the end of an old one, and it is very appropriate at such times. But it would be a pity to limit it to one part of the year, when the ideas it expresses are relevant to all of us, all the time. Like many 18th century hymns, its language is sober and restrained, appealing to the head as much as the heart. Religion generally tended to be rational rather than rapturous, a reaction against the terrible events of the previous decades, when religious sectarianism had helped plunge the country into civil war. 'Enthusiasm' was very suspect, and faith was practical rather than emotional.

But Philip Doddridge, though a man of his time in that respect, won hearts as well as minds by the warmth and humanity of his preaching and writing. His faith was of the heart, as we can see in this hymn. It is a testimony to his experience of God, which had been tested in the fire: of his nine children only four survived till adulthood, the first, Elizabeth, dying just before her fifth birthday. But he can still write:

> *By day, by night, at home, abroad,*
> *Still are we guarded by our God,*
> *By his incessant bounty fed,*
> *By his unerring counsel led.*

It is hard to think of any hymn which has better expressed the Christian's need to trust in God. In Doddridge's day life was even more uncertain than it is in our own; we have far more control over our lives than anyone did 300 years ago. But we are all still vulnerable to what Shakespeare calls 'the heartaches and the thousand natural shocks/ that flesh is heir to'. Learning to lean on God is a spiritual discipline we all need to acquire. So, says the hymn:

> *With grateful hearts the past we own;*
> *The future, all to us unknown,*
> *We to thy guardian care commit,*
> *And peaceful leave before thy feet.*

Doddridge's talents drew the attention of the Nonconformist world, and he found himself loaded not just with honours but with work, which proved in the end too much for him. He died of tuberculosis in Lisbon, where he had gone for his health, and this hymn was published after his death.

Doddridge's church in Northampton, Castle Hill United Reformed Church, still stands, but his enduring legacy lies in the hymns we still sing.

Great is thy faithfulness, O God my Father;
There is no shadow of turning with thee;
Thou changest not, thy compassions, they fail not;
As thou hast been, thou forever will be.

Great is thy faithfulness!
Great is thy faithfulness!
Morning by morning new mercies I see.
All I have needed thy hand hath provided;
Great is thy faithfulness, Lord, unto me!

✣

Great is thy faithfulness

SOME hymns are wonderful poetry, too. Others become part of our lives because they say exactly what we believe, in a way which lifts our hearts.

Great is thy faithfulness is of the latter kind. It does not stretch us with profound insights and make us see the world in a new way. Instead, it takes one simple theme – the faithfulness of God – and elaborates it through three verses and a chorus.

It was written by Thomas Chisholm, and first appeared in *Songs of Salvation and Service* in 1923. The compiler, William Runyan, wrote the tune especially for it, later recording, 'This particular poem held such an appeal that I prayed most earnestly that my tune might carry its message in a worthy way.' The hymn is a wonderful example of answered prayer. It is one of the most popular in the evangelical Protestant tradition, and it is sung all over the world.

Chisholm himself was briefly a Methodist minister, who became ill and left the ministry, eventually becoming an insurance salesman. He wrote more than 1,200 poems, many of which became hymns; this is by far his most popular. He died in 1960 at the age of 94.

The theme is suggested by Lamentations 3. 22-23, but anyone who goes to those verses for its context will find a much darker scenario than the hymn suggests. The book is what its title says – Lamentations for the terrible things faced by the people of God. When the writer says, that 'the Lord's compassions never fail, they are new every morning,' he has just painted a horrific picture of starvation, which it is hard to read even today.

Great is thy faithfulness is a cheerful, sunny hymn. We are unlikely to turn to it in our deepest distress, as we might to some others – *O love that wilt not let me go*, for instance. But that does not mean it is not true, in spite of the distance it has come from its biblical origins. Someone has said, 'Never doubt in the darkness what God has shown you in the light.' If, in time of need, we remember that God's faithfulness is very great, Chisholm and Runyan will have done their work well.

It is sometimes sung in a painfully modernised version as, 'Great is your faithfulness,' and so on. Some hymns can be updated fairly easily, and do not lose by it; tweaking the odd word or phrase allows it to speak more clearly to a different age. Others, particularly those which are not great verse to begin with, are best left as as they are. The slight archaisms disguise their weaknesses, and prolong their lives rather than shortening them.

Guide me, O thou great Jehovah,
Pilgrim through this barren land.
I am weak, but thou art mighty;
Hold me with thy powerful hand.
Bread of heaven, bread of heaven,
Feed me till I want no more;
Feed me till I want no more.

Open now the crystal fountain,
Whence the healing stream doth flow;
Let the fire and cloudy pillar
Lead me all my journey through.
Strong deliverer, strong deliverer,
Be thou still my strength and shield;
Be thou still my strength and shield.

When I tread the verge of Jordan,
Bid my anxious fears subside;
Death of death and hell's destruction,
Land me safe on Canaan's side.
Songs of praises, songs of praises,
I will ever give to thee;
I will ever give to thee.

Guide me, O thou great Jehovah

THIS is one of the hymns known as widely among non-churchgoers as among churchgoers, at least those who are rugby and football fans. However, to Christians *Guide me, O thou great Jehovah* (or, *Redeemer*) is a powerful statement of faith in a God who, whatever befalls us, preserves and protects us to the end.

It was first published in 1745 in a collection by William Williams, 'the sweet singer of Wales' (1717-1791) known as Pantycelyn from his home in Carmarthenshire. He was deeply affected by the Methodist revival movement, becoming one of its key leaders and one of the most significant of Welsh hymnwriters. He served as a travelling evangelist and was very popular as a preacher; for 43 years he travelled on average 2,230 miles a year.

The hymn originally had five verses, but is best known to English speakers in the translation by Peter Williams, a contemporary of Pantycelyn and fellow Methodist. William Williams then made his own translation, retaining Peter's first verse.

Its imagery has a powerful simplicity about it. There is nothing pretentious or forced in the English that most readers will sing. This is verse from the heart, and every word of every line is meant. It is Welsh mountain language, craggy and rough-hewn. The poet is a 'pilgrim through this barren land' – in 1745 the rocky cliffs and peaks and stony ground of the Welsh hills, not the blasted industrial landscape of the 19th and 20th century. 'I am weak, but thou art mighty,' he sings; 'hold me with thy powerful hand.'

The hymn is soaked in scripture, mainly from the book of Exodus. The stories of the wandering Israelites are metaphors for the life of God's people today. The 'bread of heaven' is the manna which sustained them; Moses struck the rock and water flowed in the desert; the Israelites were led by a pillar of cloud by day and a pillar of fire by night. But there are other references too. In this 'barren land', the bread of heaven is also perhaps the ravens feeding the prophet Elijah (1 Kings 17). When Williams writes of 'treading the verge of Jordan' – of dying, in other words – it is likely to be Bunyan's *Pilgrim's Progress* he has in mind, not just the entry of the Israelites into the promised land. When Mr Valiant-for-Truth entered the River, he said, 'Death, where is thy sting?' 'And as he went down deeper, he said: "Grave, where is thy victory?" So he passed over, and all the trumpets sounded for him on the other side."'

The hymn is inextricably linked nowadays with the tune *Cwm Rhondda*, to which it is almost invariably sung. It comes as a surprise to realise that this was only composed in 1905, by John Hughes, for a music festival in Pontypridd. The hymn caught the passion of the Welsh Revival and became the anthem of Rhondda miners. Profoundly moving and rich in spiritual feeling, it epitomises the best of Welsh hymnody. It was sung at the service at St Paul's Cathedral celebrating the Queen's Diamond Jubilee.

Hail, thou once despised Jesus!
Hail, thou Galilean King!
Thou didst suffer to release us;
Thou didst free salvation bring.
Hail, thou agonising Saviour,
Bearer of our sin and shame,
By thy merit we find favour:
Life is given through thy name.

Paschal Lamb, by God appointed,
All our sins on thee were laid:
By almighty love anointed,
Thou hast full atonement made.
All thy people are forgiven
Through the virtue of thy blood:
Opened is the gate of heaven,
Man is reconciled to God.

Jesus, hail! enthroned in glory,
There for ever to abide;
All the heavenly hosts adore thee,
Seated at thy Father's side.
There for sinners thou art pleading:
There thou dost our place prepare;
There for ever interceding
Till in glory we appear.

Worship, honour, power and blessing
Thou art worthy to receive;
Highest praises, without ceasing,
Meet it is for us to give.
Help, ye bright angelic spirits,
Bring your sweetest, noblest lays;
Help to sing your Saviour's merits,
Help to chant Emmanuel's praise!

Hail, thou once despised Jesus

THE great drama of Easter is brought to an end not by the Resurrection, but by the Ascension. The death and resurrection of Jesus are two acts of the play, the great battle with the forces of sin and darkness and the decisive and eternal victory. But when the Roman Emperors won their battles, they would be awarded a formal Triumph, a victory parade through the streets of Rome with all the treasure and captives they had gained.

The Ascension is Jesus' Triumph, his return to the Father in glory.

Hail, thou once despised Jesus is a marvellous hymn of praise to the risen and ascended Lord. It is full of theology, with pictures drawn from the book of Revelation and Paul's letters. Jesus is the lamb who was slain, now seated at the right hand of the Father. He has made atonement for our sins, and 'ever lives to intercede for us'.

The great strength of the hymn is that it combines a deep knowledge of doctrine with a deeply scriptural imagination. It is not sentimental, but it is profoundly moving. Its power comes simply from its truth, the way it creates a picture of the majesty of Jesus.

It is surprising then that a hymn which seems so be such a poetic unity should have come about the way it did. It is usually ascribed to John Bakewell (1721-1819), a Methodist from Derbyshire who moved to London and founded a church in Greenwich. But he wrote only the first verse and the first parts of verses three and four. Verse two and the second part of verse four are by Martin Madan (1725-1790), an Anglican clergyman who founded a home for ex-prostitutes; he stopped preaching because of the controversy aroused by a book in which he advocated polygamy, arguing than it was better for women than to be driven into prostitution. The second part of verse three is by Augustus Toplady, who wrote *Rock of Ages;* he is responsible for its form as we have it now.

It is usually sung to *Hyfrydol,* one of the most popular hymn tunes, composed by Rowland Prichard in 1844 before he was 20 years old.

*Hail to the Lord's anointed,
    Great David's greater Son!
Hail in the time appointed,
His reign on earth begun!
He comes to break oppression,
To set the captive free;
To take away transgression
And rule in equity.*

*He comes with succour speedy
To those who suffer wrong;
To help the poor and needy,
And bid the weak be strong;
To give them songs for sighing,
Their darkness turn to light,
Whose souls, condemned and dying,
Were precious in his sight.*

*He shall come down like showers
Upon the fruitful earth;
And love, joy, hope, like flowers,
Spring in his path to birth.
Before him, on the mountains,
Shall peace, the herald, go,
And righteousness, in fountains,
From hill to valley flow.*

*Kings shall fall down before him,
And gold and incense bring;
All nations shall adore him,
His praise all people sing;
For he shall have dominion
O'er river, sea and shore,
Far as the eagle's pinion
Or dove's light wing can soar.*

O'er every foe victorious,
He on his throne shall rest;
From age to age more glorious,
All blessing and all blest.
The tide of time shall never
His covenant remove;
His name shall stand forever,
His changeless name of love.

Hail to the Lord's Anointed

HAIL to the Lord's Anointed is usually sung now as an Advent hymn, but was first sung on Christmas Day 1821. It is a version of Psalm 72, but it is far more than just an exercise in versification.

James Montgomery (1771-1854), its author, was a prolific hymn-writer, many of whose verses are still sung today. Perhaps the best-known, apart from this one, is *Angels from the Realm of Glory*.

Born in Scotland into the Moravian faith, his parents were sent as missionaries to the West Indies when he was 12 and soon died there. Young James was apprenticed as a baker, but soon left and scraped a precarious living before working for the editor of the *Sheffield Register*. This was also a precarious living in those days of political repression. When the editor fled the country to avoid prosecution, James took over and edited it as the *Sheffield Iris* for 32 years, being himself twice imprisoned.

He left the faith of his fathers early on, but was readmitted to the Church at the age of 43, becoming an avid supporter of missions and of the Bible Society.

He was widely respected for his good works, and died unmarried aged 83.

He wrote widely, including some very perceptive – and waspish – remarks about hymn-writing. He said of some of his predecessors: 'They have begun apparently with the only idea in their mind at the time; another with little relationship to the former has been forced upon them by a refractory rhyme; a third, because necessary to eke out a verse; a fourth, to begin one; and so on.'

Montgomery's hymns, however, have a beautiful structure, with an unforced, lyrical flow of ideas. It is not easy to think of a rhyme for 'oppression' (verse 1) but you would never know it. Each verse has a logic of its own, with the last building to a wonderful theological crescendo:

> *The tide of time shall never*
> *His covenant remove;*
> *His name shall stand forever,*
> *His changeless name of love.*

'Remove' and 'love' are eye-rhymes, common at the time but not often used by Montgomery; there are various versions of the last line.

Not all his hymns are worth preserving, of course. Even in *Hail to the Lord's Anointed* there are one or two verses which are rightly left out:

> *Arabia's desert ranger*
> *To him shall bow the knee;*
> *The Ethiopian stranger*
> *His glory come to see*

sounds too quaint to modern ears.

However, this is one of those hymns which speaks to us very clearly of the majesty of the Lord Jesus Christ and his universal significance. We would probably talk about the 'cosmic Christ' today – not an expression Montgomery would have known, but another way of saying that Jesus is not just my Saviour, concerned with my small doings; he is the Saviour of the world.

It is usually sung to *Cruger*, but goes very well to *The British Grenadiers*.

*I need thee every hour, most gracious Lord;
No tender voice like thine can peace afford.*

    I need thee, O I need thee;
    Every hour I need thee;
    O bless me now, my Saviour,
    I come to thee.

*I need thee every hour; stay thou nearby;
Temptations lose their power when thou art nigh.*

*I need thee every hour, in joy or pain;
Come quickly and abide, or life is in vain.*

*I need thee every hour; teach me thy will;
And thy rich promises in me fulfill.*

*I need thee every hour, most Holy One;
O make me thine indeed, thou blessèd Son.*

I need thee every hour

THERE are surprisingly few hymns whose writers have left us an account of just how they came to be composed. We know about 'I need thee every hour' because Annie Sherwood Hawks has told us about it. In later life she wrote:

'One day as a young wife and mother of 37 years of age, I was busy with my regular household tasks. Suddenly, I became so filled with the sense of nearness to the Master that, wondering how one could live without Him, either in joy or pain, these words, "I Need Thee Every Hour," were ushered into my mind, the thought at once taking full possession of me.'

She wrote the simple couplets which form the verses of the hymn we have today and showed them to her pastor, Robert Lowry (1826-1899), a famous music editor and composer. He wrote a tune to fit the words and added the refrain, and between them they created a classic of Victorian hymnody which instantly became sung in churches everywhere.

Annie Sherwood Hawks (1836-1918) lived most of her life in New York and attended Lowry's Hanson Place Baptist Church with her husband Charles. She had written hymns since the age of 14 and was to compose more than 400 during her life, mainly for Sunday schools.

I need Thee every hour is the only one that is still widely sung today, though some of the others are very acceptable. Perhaps it is its simplicity, or perhaps the strong tune provided by Lowry with its soaring refrain of challenge and commitment.

The verses themselves express fundamental truths about the Gospel and the Christian life in a way that is almost uncomfortably direct. The Victorians on whichever side of the Atlantic were not shy of emotion; the image of the stiff-upper-lipped British empire-builder is not really a generally accurate one, though our public schools did their best to turn out such characters. In her unashamed reliance on God for every breath at every moment, Annie Hawks spoke to her time, and speaks to us today.

She was to feel the full force of her own words, 'I need Thee every hour, in joy or pain.' Sixteen years after she wrote them her beloved husband died. She wrote later: 'I did not understand at first why this hymn had touched the great throbbing heart of humanity. It was not until long after, when the shadow fell over my way, the shadow of a great loss, that I understood something of the comforting power in the words which I had been permitted to give out to others in my hour of sweet serenity and peace.'

There is a thought-provoking twist in the refrain written by Robert Lowry which is worth noticing. The verses are about our need of God. We might expect the last line of the refrain to be something like, 'O come to me.' But Lowry has us singing instead, 'I come to Thee.' The Prodigal Son has to move toward the father; Zacchaeus has to seek out Jesus; we have to want healing, and we have to take some initiative in repenting of our sins. Our relationship with God is not all take; we have to give, as well, and come willingly to him.

*I'll praise my maker while I've breath,
  And when my voice is lost in death,
Praise shall employ my nobler powers;
My days of praise shall ne'er be past,
While life, and thought, and being last,
Or immortality endures.*

*Happy the man whose hopes rely
On Israel's God: he made the sky,
And earth, and seas, with all their train:
His truth for ever stands secure;
He saves th'oppressed, he feeds the poor,
And none shall find his promise vain.*

*The Lord has eyes to give the blind;
The Lord supports the sinking mind;
He sends the labr'ing conscience peace;
He helps the stranger in distress,
The widow, and the fatherless,
And grants the pris'ner sweet release.*

*I'll praise him while he lends me breath,
And when my voice is lost in death,
Praise shall employ my nobler powers;
My days of praise shall ne'er be past,
While life, and thought, and being last,
Or immortality endures.*

I'll praise my maker while I've breath

MORE than 250 years after his death, Isaac Watts is still one of the most admired hymn-writers in the English language. Without them our language of worship would be impoverished, and his verses have provided a grammar for addressing God which few others have matched.

Born in 1674 in Southampton, Watts learned Greek, Latin and Hebrew under the local rector but entered a nonconformist academy in 1690. (In those days, so soon after the Civil War which had split the country on religious lines, Nonconformists were effectively barred from Oxford and Cambridge and still faced discrimination and persecution.)

Watts became a noted preacher and learned scholar. His poetry, as the *Dictionary of National Biography* says, 'took the religious world of dissent by storm. It gave an utterance, till then unheard in England, to the spiritual emotions, in their contemplation of God's glory in nature and his revelation in Christ, and made hymn-singing a fervid devotional force.' He wrote more than 600, of which at least 30 are still in common use.

One of them is *I'll praise my maker while I've breath*, which appeared in his *Psalms of David* collection in 1719.

A paraphrase of Psalm 146, its strength lies in the range of its thought. We are invited not only to praise God, but explore his gifts and to find reasons to praise him more. God made the sky; he saves the oppressed, he feeds the poor. He has eyes to give the blind, he supports the fainting mind. 'My days of praise shall ne'er be past,' he says, even after death – 'While life, or thought, or being last/ Or immortality endures'.

In the Peter Cook and Dudley Moore film *Bedazzled*, there's a piece where Cook (the Devil, aka George Spiggott) explains to Moore (Stanley) why he rebelled against God, telling him that it was 'the praising' that got to him. Sitting on top of a pillar box, he instructs Stanley to role-play him. 'You're so great, you're so wonderful,' says Stanley as he capers, forced after only a few moments to realise what a few millenia of such behaviour would do to the most pious of angels. But real praise is the reflection back to God in thanksgiving of the richness and complexity of a whole human life, as Watts understood very well.

I'll praise my maker is not really great verse, but not much hymnody that comes from that period is. It was, after the trauma of the Civil War, a time when 'enthusiasm' was frowned on. Many Baptist and Independent congregations became Unitarians during the 18th century, preferring its calm rationality to the dangerous doctrine of the Incarnation. But while Watts was of his time, he could still write:

When I survey the wondrous cross
Where the young prince of glory died
My richest gain I count but loss
And pour contempt on all my pride.

The Church owes him a great debt for that.

John Wesley sang the hymn when he was dying, his last words being 'I'll praise.'

Isaac Watts died in 1748.

Immortal, invisible, God only wise,
In light inaccessible hid from our eyes,
Most blessèd, most glorious, the Ancient of Days,
Almighty, victorious, thy great name we praise.

Unresting, unhasting, and silent as light,
Nor wanting, nor wasting, thou rulest in might;
Thy justice, like mountains, high soaring above
Thy clouds, which are fountains of goodness and love.

To all, life thou givest, to both great and small;
In all life thou livest, the true life of all;
We blossom and flourish as leaves on the tree,
And wither and perish – but naught changeth thee.

Great Father of glory, pure Father of light,
Thine angels adore thee, all veiling their sight;
But of all thy rich graces this grace, Lord, impart
Take the veil from our faces, the veil from our heart.

All laud we would render; O help us to see
'Tis only the splendor of light hideth thee,
And so let thy glory, Almighty, impart,
Through Christ in the story, thy Christ to the heart.

Immortal, invisible, God only wise

'NOW unto the King eternal, immortal, invisible, the only wise God, be honour and glory for ever and ever, Amen.'

This resounding expression of praise is from 1 Timothy 1. 17, and it is it the verse on which Walter Chalmers Smith (1824-1908) based his hymn *Immortal, invisible, God only wise.*

It is one of the great hymns of the 19th century, and its doctrinal orthodoxy and deep spirituality mean that is sung in every Christian tradition.

Smith was a Free Church of Scotland minister throughout his life, serving mainly in Scotland though his first pastorate was at the Chadwell Street Scottish Church in London.

He was steeped in the Bible and had a deep sense of the majesty of God. The hymn is a beautifully unforced and serene expression of awe at God's greatness. It draws on imagery from the natural world – 'Thy justice, like mountains, high soaring above/ Thy clouds, which are fountains of goodness and love' – but everything is majestic and full of wonder.

God is 'Most blessèd, most glorious, the Ancient of Days,/ Almighty, victorious ...' He is the 'Great Father of glory, pure Father of light,' whose 'angels adore Thee, all veiling their sight'.

Some hymns take as their themes God's dealings with his people and reflect the emotional and spiritual side of faith. Others deal with Kingdom issues like peace and justice. *Immortal, invisible* is focused solely on God. In this hymn, human beings are there to highlight his otherness. 'We blossom and flourish as leaves on the tree,/ And wither and perish – but naught changeth Thee.' All our human achievements are put firmly in their place; only God is eternal.

But there is a wonderful prayer at the core of the hymn. Having framed a powerful statement of God's greatness which, in spite of its link to 1 Timothy, has more in common with the Psalms, Smith brings it firmly back to the New Testament. In Exodus 34 we read of Moses, who would talk with God, and whose face would reflect a glory so bright that he would have to cover his face to prevent the Israelites from being blinded by it. In 2 Corinthians 3. 13-15, Paul says, 'We are not like Moses, who would put a veil over his face to keep the Israelites from gazing at it while the radiance was fading away ... Even to this day when Moses is read, a veil covers their hearts. But whenever anyone turns to the Lord, the veil is taken away.' In other words, it was the people's lack of capacity which prevented them experiencing the glory of God for themselves.

So the hymn asks God to 'Take the veil from our faces, the veil from our heart.' Through Christ, each one of us has access to the throne of God himself. We need not be afraid, because we have become his children. Through the mighty power of God, the Christ in the story has become Christ in our hearts.

Smith wrote several books of poems and devotional works. The only other hymn of his to remain popular is the evocative advent hymn *Earth was waiting, spent and restless*.

Immortal, invisible is usually sung to *St Denio*, based on a Welsh folk-tune and usually attributed to John Roberts (1822-1877).

*In a byre near Bethlehem
Passed by many a wandering stranger
The most precious word of life
Was heard gurgling in a manger
For the good of us all.*

*And he's here when we call him
Bringing health, love, and laughter
To life now and ever after
For the good of us all.*

In a byre near Bethlehem

THE Church's worship has been immeasurably enriched over the last few years by the songs and hymns of the Iona Community.

Its writers draw on Celtic traditions and old folk tunes, mainly Scottish, but they are rooted in the real work of the Community, whose spirituality is a launching pad for a ministry of peace, justice and healing. Many of them are very moving and evocative, but they do not take us to a misty Highland never-never land; there is an edge to them which makes them much more than that.

In a byre near Bethlehem is a good example.

John Bell and Graham Maule, who wrote it, are two marvellous wordsmiths. Oddly enough, one of the qualities which makes their work stand out is its rough, unfinished quality. It is not polished verse, all cool and controlled; it is rather awkward at times, almost as though it is a first draft rather than the product of long labour.

So for instance, the first verse has Jesus 'gurgling in a manger' – well, babies do gurgle, but in hymns they keep a dignified silence ('no crying he makes'). Does 'quiet' in the third verse 'camouflage' the priest and soldier? Not really. And does 'the grave of human violence' really make sense in the last?

But this is one of those hymns which would lose if someone tried to improve it. It takes us on a journey from the cradle to the grave, and out on the other side, all the time reminding us Jesus is 'here when we call him/ bringing health, love and laughter'. This is a very human Christ (in the Celtic tradition) who 'took the world's weight on his shoulder', and died 'for the good of us all'. Theological purists might object to this; Jesus is a bit too close, perhaps, and not divine enough. And health, love and laughter – did he have nothing to say about sin?

However, the hymn is not about that; it is about the Jesus who was good company, who was attractive and made people want to be with him. This Jesus enriched people's lives, rather than making them feel bad about themselves.

There is a beautiful image in the last verse: the 'most precious Word of life/ cleared his throat, and ended silence'. How do we envisage the Resurrection? Choirs of angels, trumpets, an explosion of power? There is far more drama in the thought of a quiet cough in a hillside cave; a man is raised from the dead as easily as we wake from sleep.

The hymn is sung to the beautiful Irish traditional melody *Wild Mountain Thyme*, which has been covered by dozens if not hundreds of artists: The Corries, Bob Dylan and Sandy Denny, among many others.

*It is a thing most wonderful,
   Almost too wonderful to be,
That God's own Son should come from heaven,
And die to save a child like me.*

*And yet I know that it is true:
He chose a poor and humble lot,
And wept, and toiled, and mourned, and died,
For love of those who loved him not.*

*I cannot tell how he would love
A child so weak and full of sin;
His love must be most wonderful,
If he could die my love to win.*

*I sometimes think about the cross,
And shut my eyes, and try to see
The cruel nails and crown of thorns
And Jesus crucified for me.*

*But even could I see him die,
I could but see a little part
Of that great love, which, like a fire,
Is always burning in his heart.*

*It is most wonderful to know
His love for me so free and sure;
But 'tis more wonderful to see
My love for him so faint and poor.*

*And yet I want to love thee, Lord;
O light the flame within my heart,
And I will love thee more and more,
Until I see thee as thou art.*

It is a thing most wonderful

THERE are perhaps two traps into which Christians can fall when thinking about the death of Christ. The first is to think altogether too much about it; to make particular doctrines about what it means and how it worked the test of orthodoxy, and get very suspicious of people who don't quite see it the same way as us. The second is not to think about it very much at all; to let it become part of the furniture of our spiritual lives, so that it recedes to the background of belief rather than being a living reality.

A hymn like *It is a thing most wonderful,* by William Walsham How (1823-97) calls us back to a healthier spirituality. It is the product of deep reflection, but also deep feeling. The death of Jesus, for him, is not first of all something to be fitted into a theological scheme; it is something at which he marvels, and which knocks him to his knees. God was in Christ, reconciling the world to himself; a man died for love of those who did not know him and did not care about him.

It is this sense of baffled awe which is at the heart of devotion, and which How expresses so well. This is 'almost too wonderful to be', he says in the first verse, though he adds, 'And yet I know that it is true.' It is a deeply personal meditation:

> *I cannot tell how he could love*
> *A child so weak and full of sin*
> *His love must be most wonderful*
> *If he could die my love to win.*

There is a note of melancholy realism in it as well; he says:

> *It is most wonderful to know*
> *His love for me so free and sure*
> *But 'tis more wonderful to know*
> *My love for him so faint and poor.*

It closes with a prayer, that God will 'teach me how to grow in grace/ And I will love thee more and more/ Until I see thee face to face.'

It is a thing most wonderful is one of those hymns which bring together deep feeling and intense spirituality with real theological insight. It is also very accomplished as verse, without any attempt at verbal fireworks or intricate rhyming schemes. It reads almost as though How is thinking aloud, jotting down his musings as they came to him. But you have to be a very good writer indeed to produce something that flows so well, in which there is not a wasted word, where every rhyme is natural and right, and in which all of us believers can recognise our own experience. We do not understand the depth of Christ's love for us; we do not love him enough in return; we wish we did, and one day we will.

William Walsham How was an Anglican clergyman who became the first Bishop of Wakefield; there is a marble memorial to him in the cathedral there, though he is buried in Whittington, Shropshire, where he was rector for 28 years after curacies in Kidderminster and Shrewsbury. He also served as suffragan Bishop of London.

How was highly regarded for the concern he showed for industrial workers and the poor.

He wrote many hymns, including *For all the saints, O Jesus, thou art standing*, and *O word of God incarnate*, which are still popular today.

Jesus lives! thy terrors now
Can, O death, no more appall us;
Jesus lives! by this we know
Thou, O grave, canst not enthrall us.
Alleluia!

Jesus lives! henceforth is death
But the gate of life immortal;
This shall calm our trembling breath
When we pass its gloomy portal.
Alleluia!

Jesus lives! for us he died;
Then, alone to Jesus living,
Pure in heart may we abide,
Glory to our Saviour giving.
Alleluia!

Jesus lives! our hearts know well
Nought from us his love shall sever;
Life, nor death, nor powers of hell
Tear us from his keeping ever.
Alleluia!

Jesus lives! to him the throne
Over all the world is given:
May we go where he has gone,
Rest and reign with him in heaven.
Alleluia!

Jesus lives!

EASTER is a time for joyful, triumphant music, with words that express the full pageant of salvation and redemption. Over the centuries the Church's great hymn-writers have produced many wonderful expressions of thanksgiving to enrich the worship of this time. They help us rise to the occasion, and give us the language to praise God as we ought.

One of these is Jesus lives! by Christian Fürchtegott Gellert (1715-1769). It is a deceptively simple but profound assertion of the lordship of Christ in the face of death. Death is mentioned in every verse except the last, but each ends with an *Alleluia!*

Gellert studied theology at the University of Leipzig, and then served as an assistant to his father, the pastor at Hainichen. He was very shy and had poor health, and felt that that made him unsuited for the ministry. He became a tutor, and eventually a professor of philosophy at his old University, where he was universally popular. He wrote many articles, poems and novels, as well as hymns – and the hymns were equally admired by both Protestants and Catholics, unusually for the time.

Jesus lives! is an Easter hymn which is very clear about the spiritual and theological significance of the Resurrection. It means that death has been conquered.

Death is universal, but previous generations lived much closer to death than we do today. We are used, perhaps, to arguing for Christianity on the grounds that it makes sense of life, or that we can have a knowledge of God, or that Christian faith offers the best hope for making the world a better place. All these things are true, but they are not really at the heart of what the Resurrection means – and it was the Resurrection which Paul preached in Athens, and which has drawn countless men and women to faith over the years. The Resurrection means that those who believe will never die; that beyond the grave there is a new, bright and glorious life.

Christian Gellert knew this and expressed it simply and powerfully.

> *Jesus lives! Thy terrors now*
> *Can, O death, no more appal us;*
> *Jesus lives! By this we know,*
> *Thou, O grave, canst not enthral us.*

Death, he says, is now 'but the gate of life immortal'. Nothing shall keep us from the love of Christ, he says in verse four, echoing Romans 8 – 'Life, nor death, nor powers of hell,/ Tear us from his keeping ever.' And just to remind us that there is more than our own salvation at stake, he concludes 'Jesus lives! To him the throne/ Over all the world is given ...' Christ is Lord of all.

Jesus lives! is sung to several tunes. One very appropriate one is *St Albinus*, by the influential composer and organ designer Henry John Gauntlett (1805-1876). He is credited with inventing the four-part style of hymn tunes, and with introducing electric pumps to power organs.

Jesus shall reign where e'er the sun
Doth his successive journeys run;
His kingdom stretch from shore to shore,
Till moons shall wax and wane no more.

To him shall endless prayer be made,
And praises throng to crown his head;
His name like sweet perfume shall rise
With every morning sacrifice.

People and realms of every tongue
Dwell on his love with sweetest song;
And infant voices shall proclaim
Ttheir early blessings on his name.

Blessings abound where e'er he reigns:
Tthe prisoner leaps to lose his chains,
The weary find eternal rest,
And all the sons of want are blest.

Let every creature rise and bring
Peculiar honours to our King;
Angels descend with songs again,
And earth repeat the loud Amen.

Jesus shall reign

WE are so used to singing all kinds of songs and hymns in worship that it is hard to think of it as ever being controversial. But in the 17th and 18th centuries the early Nonconformists would only sing Psalms.

Then came Isaac Watts (1674-1748), known as the 'father of English hymnody'. A prolific writer, theologian and preacher, he wrote hymns based on personal experience, teaching doctrine from the heart as well as from the textbook.

Of the 750 he is credited with, a good few are still sung, including *Jesus shall reign where'er the sun*. Usually today we sing five or six verses; the original had 14, including some which are rather quaint to modern ears – like:

> *There Persia, glorious to behold,*
> *There India shines in eastern gold;*
> *And barb'rous nations at his word*
> *Submit, and bow, and own their Lord.*

That verse, though, is a good summary of what the hymn is about. It celebrates the lordship of Christ over all the world. In an age when Christendom was comfortably European, Watts dared to assert his rule over the whole earth. It is a millennial vision, based on the teachings of Paul in Colossians and Philippians, and on the book of Revelation. Christ's reign will be completed in God's time, in a future which may be near or distant but is in God's gift.

But it also reflects on our present experience: 'Blessings abound where'er he reigns/ The prisoner leaps to lose his chains ...' This is not just a future promise, it is a present reality. God does this for people now.

It is a deeply Christian hymn, but it is based firmly on Psalm 72 – which does not mention Christ at all. This is in keeping with Watts's view of the Old Testament, that it pointed to Christ. So he believed that the Psalms should be 'renovated', as one writer describes it; the title of his 1719 metrical psalter refers to them being 'imitated in the language of the New Testament'.

Nowadays, we are very conscious of the need to be sensitive to other religions; dialogue is important, and it is worth asking ourselves what a Muslim or a Hindu might feel when listening to a hymn like this. Jesus's kingdom 'shall stretch from shore to shore' – a line like this might very well be seen as a declaration of hostilities. That is no reason for us not to sing it, but as we do so we might want to think about how we approach those of other faiths, or of none. Are they an enemy to overcome, or someone God wants to bring into his family of faith, or someone who should be respected for living in the light God has given them?

Jesus, lover of my soul,
  Let me to thy bosom fly,
While the nearer waters roll,
While the tempest still is high.
Hide me, O my Saviour, hide,
Till the storm of life is past;
Safe into the haven guide;
O receive my soul at last.

Other refuge have I none,
hangs my helpless soul on thee;
Leave, ah! leave me not alone,
Still support and comfort me.
All my trust on thee is stayed,
All my help from thee I bring;
Cover my defenceless head
With the shadow of thy wing.

Thou, O Christ, art all I want,
More than all in thee I find;
Raise the fallen, cheer the faint,
Heal the sick, and lead the blind.
Just and holy is thy name,
I am all unrighteousness;
False and full of sin I am;
Thou art full of truth and grace.

Plenteous grace with thee is found,
Grace to cover all my sin;
Let the healing streams abound;
Make and keep me pure within.
Thou of life the fountain art,
Freely let me take of thee;
Spring thou up within my heart;
Rise to all eternity.

Jesus, lover of my soul,

CHARLES Wesley (1707-1788) is one of the greatest hymn-writers in the English language – Methodists would claim that he is the greatest! Certainly no other writer of the 18th century has so many hymns still used in worship today. His phrases, his theology and his spirituality have had more influence on particularly Nonconformist religion than anything else apart from the Bible.

This hymn appeared in his *Hymns and Sacred Poems* in 1740. One tradition says that it was written after Charles had a narrow escape from a mob in Killyleagh, County Down. They objected to his preaching salvation by grace, and he had to take refuge under a hedge until the danger was over. Perhaps this brings a new insight to the words, 'Hide me, O my Saviour, hide/ Till the storm of life is past.'

Another story – and this was told to me many years ago by one who was there – relates to the days when Welsh pubs closed on Sundays, and there would be what we might now call 'booze cruises' from Cardiff to Weston-super-Mare. Hard-drinking men would spend the day in the English pubs, and catch the last ferry home at night. All the way across the Severn they would sing rowdy drinking songs, but as they came into the harbour they would fall silent before striking up *Jesus, lover of my soul,* with its haunting line, 'Safe into the haven guide/ O receive my soul at last.'

Methodist hymns were often mocked by the 'High and Dry' Anglicans of the 18th century for being over-emotional. This is one which might have attracted their scorn – it has honest, passionate appeals to Jesus for rescue and help, it calls on him to 'cover my defenceless head/ with the shadow of thy wing'. And it calls Jesus the 'lover of my soul' – the language of experience, not of cold reason.

But this hymn is a world away from the trite nonsense which many song-writers put out today – not forgetting that there were many bad writers in Wesley's day, too. It is full of thought, as well as feeling.

Charles is honest about his sense of abandonment and unworthiness, and of the holiness of God – 'False and full of sin I am/ Thou art full of truth and grace'.

Above all, he has a clear and wonderful sense of God's goodness and his power to save.

> *Plenteous grace with thee is found,*
> *Grace to cover all my sin;*
> *Let the healing streams abound,*
> *Make and keep me pure within*

– these are biblical ideas expressed in a beautifully concise and lyrical way. Notice the prayer to be kept pure – perfectibility was a Wesleyan emphasis.

It is a hymn we love to sing, because it expresses our own longings, failures, and need for rescue. We sense that Charles Wesley's Jesus is real, and that he loves us, too.

The hymn is sometimes sung to JB Dykes' tune *Hollingside*, but compared with the best-known setting *Aberystwyth* – which is what would have drifted over Cardiff Bay on Sunday evenings – that one is rather dull.

Just as I am, without one plea,
But that thy blood was shed for me,
And that thou bidst me come to thee,
O Lamb of God, I come, I come.

Just as I am, and waiting not
To rid my soul of one dark blot,
To thee whose blood can cleanse each spot,
O Lamb of God, I come, I come.

Just as I am, though tossed about
With many a conflict, many a doubt,
Fightings and fears within, without,
O Lamb of God, I come, I come.

Just as I am, poor, wretched, blind;
Sight, riches, healing of the mind,
Yea, all I need in thee to find,
O Lamb of God, I come, I come.

Just as I am, thou wilt receive,
Wilt welcome, pardon, cleanse, relieve;
Because thy promise I believe,
O Lamb of God, I come, I come.

Just as I am, thy love unknown
Hath broken every barrier down;
Now, to be thine, yea thine alone,
O Lamb of God, I come, I come.

Just as I am

ONE of the great evangelical hymns of the 19th century has lasted into the 21st, and its usefulness is far from over.

Just as I am expresses a profound truth in simple but powerful language. Its unifying idea is grace; there is nothing we can do to make us acceptable to God, and we do not have to wait until we are good enough to come to him, because we never will be. So in churches which practise believers' baptism, it is often used as a baptismal hymn; it has a place – though decreasingly so, probably – at evangelistic services; and it feeds the devotion of Christians who know that they are welcomed by God not because of who they are, but in spite of it.

It was written by Charlotte Elliott in 1835. She became an invalid at the age of 30, and suffered ill-health for the rest of her long life (she died at the age of 82). We do not know the nature of the illness, but she wrote of it 'My Heavenly Father knows, and He alone, what it is, day after day, and hour after hour, to fight against bodily feelings of almost overpowering weakness and languor and exhaustion, to resolve, as He enables me to do, not to yield to the slothfulness, the depression, the irritability, such as a body causes me to long to indulge ...'

She was converted after visiting friends in the West End of London, and meeting there a minister, Cesar Malan. While they were eating supper he asked if she were a Christian; irritable from the pain of her illness, she said she did not wish to discuss it. But the question preyed on her mind, and when they met again she said 'I am miserable. I want to be saved. I want to come to Jesus; but I don't know how.' 'Why not come just as you are?' answered Malan. You have only to come to Him just as you are.'

The words may have been given to her then, but the hymn came later. According to Bishop H C G Moule of Durham, who was related to her, she was deeply troubled by her seeming uselessness. This feeling came to a point in 1834, when she was 45 and her brother, a minister, was deeply involved in raising funds to set up a school. A bazaar was planned, and the whole house was busily making preparations – except Charlotte, who was unwell. She lay awake all night, but in the morning realised that her sense of being good for nothing was a spiritual assault, which had to be met by an appeal to the promises of God.

So while the rest of the household was busy at the bazaar, she wrote *Just as I am*. Perhaps in some of its lines – 'Just as I am, though tossed about/ With many a conflict, many a doubt' and 'Just as I am, poor, wretched, blind' we can hear echoes of her own situation. But the hymn takes its enduring value from the fact that it speaks for all of us:

Just as I am, thou wilt receive,
Wilt welcome, pardon, cleanse, relieve,
Because thy promise I believe:
O Lamb of God, I come.

The last line of each verse is hypnotic in its intensity. It was used during the altar calls at the Billy Graham crusades, and has probably accompanied more souls to salvation than any other hymn ever written.

*King of glory, King of peace,
  I will love thee;
And that love may never cease,
I will move thee.
Thou hast granted my request,
Thou hast heard me;
Thou didst note my working breast,
Thou hast spared me.*

*Wherefore with my utmost art
I will sing thee,
And the cream of all my heart
I will bring thee.
Though my sins against me cried,
Thou didst clear me;
And alone, when they replied,
Thou didst hear me.*

*Seven whole days, not one in seven,
I will praise thee;
In my heart, though not in heaven,
I can raise thee.
Small it is, in this poor sort
To enrol thee:
E'en eternity's too short
To extol thee.*

King of glory, King of peace

SOME hymns are good poetry too; some poetry makes great hymns.

George Herbert (1593-1632) was an Anglican priest who is greatly honoured by the Church of England today for his saintly life, practical wisdom and integrity in his calling. His example – faithfully visiting his flock, devoting himself to their service and taking responsibility for the spiritual condition of his parish – is not always regarded as particularly helpful as a model of ministry today by hard-pressed Anglican clergy. They operate in a very different world, but George Herbert's influence has been a very healthy one over the centuries.

He wrote poetry, not hymns, but some of his poems have been very successfully set to music. *King of glory, King of peace* is a lovely song of praise which is deceptively simple. It is darker than we sometimes imagine. Its first verse is the record of spiritual trouble: 'King of glory, King of peace,/ I will love Thee,' he says – it is an act of will, not a natural emotion. He prays that 'love may never cease', fearing that it will; the 'working breast' is an expression of profound spiritual unease. Herbert himself wrote to his friend Nicholas Ferrar that his writings were 'a picture of spiritual conflicts between God and my soul before I could subject my will to Jesus, my Master'.

The second verse moves from struggle to faith: he will bring God 'the cream of all my heart'. He has been forgiven and loved. In the third verse we almost hear the bells of Bemerton, his church in Wiltshire, ringing out the rhythm of the words:

> *Seven whole days, not one in seven,*
> *I will praise Thee;*
> *In my heart, though not in Heaven,*
> *I can raise Thee.*
> *Small it is, in this poor sort*
> *To enrol Thee:*
> *E'en eternity's too short*
> *To extol Thee.*

'In my heart, though not in heaven/ I can raise thee' means that God in heaven is beyond praise, but that the Christian can worship him on earth. 'Enrol' is used in the sense of 'celebrate'.

His belief in praising God 'seven whole days, not one in seven' is fundamental to Christian discipleship. We are Christians all the time, and we are never off duty. Integrity is what we do when no one is watching.

George Herbert's integrity as a pastor made him celebrated after his short and quite obscure life had run its course. He died aged only 39, having been a priest only three years. Izaak Walton – who also wrote *The Compleat Angler,* a famous book about fishing – wrote his biography and made him more widely known.

The Puritan pastor Richard Baxter wrote of him, 'Herbert speaks to God like one that really believeth a God, and whose business in the world is most with God. Heart-work and heaven-work make up his books.'

When he was dying he had his poems sent to Nicholas Ferrar at Little Gidding, saying: 'Desire him to read it, and then, if he can think it may turn to the advantage of any dejected poor soul, let it be made public; if not let him burn it; for I and it are less than the least of God's mercies.'

King of Glory is usually sung to *Gwalchmai*, by Joseph David Jones (1827-1870). Born in rural Wales, he had little formal schooling but was a gifted musician who earned enough from his writing to attend college in London.

*L*ead us, heavenly Father, lead us
  O'er the world's tempestuous sea;
Guard us, guide us, keep us, feed us,
For we have no help but thee:
Yet possessing
Every blessing,
If our God our Father be.

Saviour, breathe forgiveness o'er us;
All our weakness thou dost know;
Thou didst tread this earth before us;
Thou didst feel its keenest woe;
Lone and dreary,
Faint and weary,
Through the desert thou didst go.

Spirit of our God, descending,
Fill our hearts with heavenly joy;
Love with every passion blending,
Pleasure that can never cloy:
Thus provided,
Pardoned, guided,
Nothing can our peace destroy.

Lead us, heavenly Father, lead us

RARELY, hymns are almost-perfect combinations of good theology, spiritual insight and liturgical awareness. As well as getting their doctrine right, they teach us about ourselves and our walk with God, and are ideal for particular parts of a service.

Lead us, heavenly Father, lead us is one of them. Written by James Edmeston (1791-1867), it is a Trinitarian hymn to the three persons of the Godhead.

In some hands this sort of hymn can be rather too easy. They allow the writer to produce single verses on unconnected themes, with a structure provided by the Father, Son and Spirit progression rather than by any real internal development. James Edmeston manages to say different things in each verse while maintaining a sense of artistic unity.

God the Father is the keeper and guide. The reference to the sea is not really a biblical one (the Hebrews were not seafarers) but the theme echoes the wandering in the wilderness, led by the pillar of cloud and the pillar of fire. In Bible times the sea stood for chaos, everything that was opposed to the will of God; not a bad way of thinking about the shape life takes for many of us. But we possess every blessing we need, knowing that God is our Father.

The second verse picks up a theme Edmeston deals with in other hymns – that Christ walked our paths and lived a human life. 'Thou didst tread this earth before us,/ Thou didst feel its keenest woe.'

In another hymn he says:

> *As oft, with worn and weary feet,*
> *We tread earth's rugged valley o'er,*
> *The thought, how comforting and sweet:*
> *Christ trod this very path before!*
> *Our wants and weaknesses he knows,*
> *From life's first dawning to its close.*

There is a very precious truth here: as the writer to the Hebrews says, we have a High Priest who is able to sympathise with our weaknesses.

The final verse lifts up our minds and hearts to heaven, and finishes on a note of glad praise:

'Spirit of our God descending/ Fill our hearts with heavenly joy ...'

This is a wonderful hymn to sing at the end of a service. It sums up what we should have received from God and given to him in worship: acknowledging him as Lord and Father, identifying with the Crucified Lord Jesus, and being given strength for our Christian pilgrimage through the Spirit.

James Edmeston was an architect and surveyor who served as churchwarden at Homerton, Middlesex, where he died. He was a great supporter of the London Orphan Asylum, and wrote around 2,000 hymns. Very few of them have survived, but *Lead us, heavenly Father* deserves to be remembered and sung.

It is usually sung to *Mannheim*, by Friedrich Filitz (1804-1876), a music critic and historian who worked in Berlin and Munich.

*L*ord *of all hopefulness, Lord of all joy,*
Whose trust, ever child-like, no cares could destroy,
Be there at our waking, and give us, we pray,
Your bliss in our hearts, Lord, at the break of the day.

Lord of all hopefulness

JAN Struther (1901-1953) was the pen-name of Joyce Anstruther, or Joyce Maxtone Grahame as she was for much of her life. She wrote *Lord of all hopefulness*, her best-known hymn, at the request of Canon Percy Dearmer of Westminster Abbey. However, it is not as a hymn-writer that she is principally remembered, but as the author of a famous wartime morale-booster, *Mrs Miniver*. Made into a film starring Greer Garson as the heroine, it began life as a series of columns in *Punch*, whose editor Peter Fleming had asked to write about 'an ordinary sort of woman who leads an ordinary sort of life – rather like yourself'.

She was not, in fact, ordinary at all. Joyce Anstruther was a considerable beauty, who had shared a classroom with the future Queen Mother, whose pigtails she once dipped in ink. She was an accomplished writer with a great zest for life. But *Mrs Miniver* served its purpose: it portrays a middle-class woman 'carrying on' in the face of wartime privations, managing home and family and still keeping cheerful. US president Franklin D Roosevelt told her that *Mrs Miniver* had considerably hastened America's entry into the war; and Winston Churchill said that the book had done more for the Allies than a flotilla of battleships.

Jan Struther was not conventionally religious, and was not a willing churchgoer. Indeed she once said to Percy Dearmer, 'My dear Percy, don't tell me you really believe all this stuff!'

But *Lord of all hopefulness* is more than just a technical exercise written to please a friend. It has the ring of truth about it, because it brings the life of Jesus into relation with our own lives. And this is very much a product of the author's own impatience with dogma: she lived through experience, not through ideas, and a Jesus like us was much more attractive to her than the theologian's learned theories.

The hymn works on different levels. Read one way, it is a hymn for a day: we wake up, we go to work, we come home, we sleep. All of these activities have their appropriate sentiments: hopefulness and joy in the morning, gentleness and calm at night. And they echo the life of Jesus, who experienced human life as we do, and knows us intimately because of it.

But the hymn also speaks of the stages of our lives, from childhood, to adulthood, to old age and death. So the hopefulness and joy of the first verse are characteristic of childhood. The eagerness and faith are what we offer in the strength of our maturity; kindliness and grace are the gifts of age, and gentleness and calm are what we pray for as we approach our end. In all these, Christ is there.

Whatever Jan Struther's theology, it is very hard to believe that she wrote these words without meaning them. In any case, they are a precious gift of God to his Church, and they will continue to bless to his people for many years to come.

It is sung to *Slane*, a traditional Irish melody.

Love divine, all loves excelling,
Joy of heaven to earth come down;
Fix in us thy humble dwelling;
All thy faithful mercies crown!
Jesus, thou art all compassion,
Pure unbounded love thou art;
Visit us with thy salvation;
Enter every trembling heart.

Breathe, O breathe thy loving Spirit,
Into every troubled breast!
Let us all in thee inherit;
Let us find thy promised rest.
Take away the love of sinning;
Alpha and Omega be;
End of faith, as its beginning,
Set our hearts at liberty.

Come, Almighty to deliver,
Let us all thy grace receive;
Suddenly return and never,
Never more thy temples leave.
Thee we would be always blessing,
Serve thee as thy hosts above,
Pray and praise thee without ceasing,
Glory in thy perfect love.

Finish, then, thy new creation;
Pure and spotless let us be.
Let us see thy great salvation
Perfectly restored in thee;
Changed from glory into glory,
Till in heaven we take our place,
Till we cast our crowns before thee,
Lost in wonder, love, and praise.

Love divine

CHARLES Wesley was undoubtedly one of the most prolific hymn-writers ever, having produced more than 6,000 during his lifetime. Most of them are not sung any more – Wesley had a fair number of misses among his hits – but a good number are.

Among these are some which rank among the greatest hymns ever written, in that they bring together sound doctrine, spiritual wisdom, evangelical passion, poetic flair, and an instinct for what congregations can do with their voices.

Love divine, all loves excelling is sung in almost every Christian tradition in the English-speaking world. It is very densely written, full of theology, but with a real feeling of devotion too.

Its theme is the indwelling of God in the heart of the believer. As such, it is really a hymn about the Spirit; Jesus is addressed in the first verse – 'thou art all compassion' – and asked to 'breathe thy loving Spirit/ into every troubled breast' in the second. (At least one modern hymn-book omits this verse, destroying the theological sense of the hymn.) The idea is from the Apostle Paul, who wrote, 'Do you not know that your body is a temple of the Holy Spirit, who is in you, whom you have received from God? (1 Corinthians 6. 19) and 'We are the temple of the Living God' (2 Corinthians 6. 18).

Like many old hymns, this one has been modernised by some hymn book compilers to remove the archaic language. Of course, there is nothing wrong in principle with this, and a little judicious tinkering can preserve a good hymn for modern use. It has to be done very carefully, though. In one version, 'Jesus, thou art all compassion/ Pure, unbounded love thou art' becomes, 'Jesus, you are all compassion/Boundless love that makes us whole.' The second version shifts the focus from Jesus to us; the concern with 'wholeness' is a very modern preoccupation. But once 'trembling heart' is changed to 'trembling soul', a rhyme must be found somehow.

Love divine also speaks of Wesley's belief in the doctrine of Christian perfection. This is not quite the same as sinlessness; but it is, according to Charles' brother John, 'the mind which was in Christ, enabling us to walk as Christ walked', 'purity of intention, dedicating all the life to God'. This, he believed, was achievable through prayer and self-discipline.

This doctrine is contained in the second verse, with the lines, 'Let us find that second (or 'promised') rest' (that is, when we no longer wish to sin) and 'Take away our bent to sinning (or, 'love of sinning') ...'

Many Christians today would be uncomfortable with the idea of perfectionism, being all too familiar with their own shortcomings. But it is still a good prayer to pray, and it does not really take away from one of the most glorious hymns in the language.

Love divine is usually sung to *Blaenwern*, by William Rowlands, though a number of other tunes are also popular.

*L*ord, make me an instrument of your peace,
Where there is hatred, let me sow love;
Where there is injury, pardon;
Where there is doubt, faith;
Where there is despair, hope;
Where there is darkness, light;
Where there is sadness, joy.

O Divine Master,
grant that I may not so much seek to be consoled, as to console;
to be understood, as to understand;
to be loved, as to love.
For it is in giving that we receive.
It is in pardoning that we are pardoned,
and it is in dying that we are born to eternal life.
Amen.

✣

Make me a channel of your peace

IT is one of the best-known of all modern hymns, with inspirational words and a dignified, meditative but melodic tune. It is sung by the Royal British Legion at its annual Festival of Remembrance in the Royal Albert Hall, and it is a moving expression of total spiritual commitment.

Sebastian Temple's *Make me a channel of your peace* is closely based on the Prayer of St Francis, a reference to the 13th century Francis of Assisi. Francis was an Italian nobleman who felt God calling him to 'repair his house'. He came to see that this meant reforming the Church, not in its structures or doctrine but in its devotion to Christ. Gathering a group of followers around him, he devoted himself to the poor and to prayer, giving up all his own worldly possessions and witnessing to the love of Christ in deeds as well as in words.

Unfortunately, however well the Prayer expresses the teachings of Francis, he certainly did not write it and it is not even decently mediaeval. Its earliest appearance was as an anonymous piece in December 1912, in a small French devotional magazine called *La Clochette (The Little Bell)*. It was later sent to Pope Benedict XV, who had it translated into Italian and published in the official Vatican newspaper *L'Osservatore Romano* in January 1916, while the world was in the throes of the Great War.

So it first found popularity as a prayer for peace, and it gains an added layer of meaning as we remember that. 'Where there is hatred let me bring your love' and 'Where there's despair in life let me bring hope' have a particular poignancy today. International tensions are rising and the world is facing seemingly insoluble problems. While we might like to think of the hymn as about personal relationships and individual trials, it is much more than that.

It is, too, very ambitious in its spiritual reach, and not to be sung lightly. Asking God to make us channels of his peace commits us to a very costly discipleship. The chorus is particularly hard: we all want to be consoled, to be understood, and to be loved, but we pray that we will be able to lay these natural human desires aside for the sake of others. Here in a few lines we have the eternal conflict between the absolute call of God upon our lives, and our need to function as normal people who have friends, families, work and all sorts of other calls on us. We are not all called to be barefoot friars like Francis; most of us need to find our way to a rounded discipleship.

The song can be overused. When it is sung properly the tune is lovely, but it can be a bit of a dirge if not. And its popularity in school assemblies means that it appears rather frequently at weddings, as one of the few hymns non-churchgoers can actually remember; it is not particularly appropriate on such occasions.

The prayer itself was famously quoted by Margaret Thatcher on the steps of 10 Downing Street as she took up office as prime minister. Whatever the achievements of her government, her hope that it would bring harmony in place of discord were notably unfulfilled. For better or worse, it was the beginning of the most divisive period of British political life since the war.

It came upon the midnight clear,
That glorious song of old,
From angels bending near the earth,
To touch their harps of gold;
'Peace on the earth, good will to men,
From heaven's all gracious king.'
The world in solemn stillness lay,
To hear the angels sing.

Still through the cloven skies they come
With peaceful wings unfurled,
And still their heavenly music floats
O'er all the weary world;
Above its sad and lowly plains,
They bend on hovering wing,
And ever over its Babel sounds
The blessèd angels sing.

Yet with the woes of sin and strife
The world has suffered long;
Beneath the angel strain have rolled
Two thousand years of wrong;
And man, at war with man, hears not
The love-song which they bring;
O hush the noise, ye men of strife
And hear the angels sing.

And ye, beneath life's crushing load,
Whose forms are bending low,
Who toil along the climbing way
With painful steps and slow,
Look now! for glad and golden hours
Come swiftly on the wing.
O rest beside the weary road,
And hear the angels sing!

For lo! the days are hastening on,
By prophet-bards foretold,
When with the ever circling years
Comes round the age of gold;
When peace shall over all the earth
Its ancient splendours fling,
And the whole world send back the song
Which now the angels sing.

It came upon the midnight clear

THIS hymn is a Christmas favourite among many orthodox Christians. The 'angels bending near the earth/ To touch their harps of gold', coming through the cloven skies 'with peaceful wings unfurled', bending on hovering wing to sing of the Messiah's birth; it is all wonderful imagery, and Christmas wouldn't be the same without it.

It might come as a surprise then to know that the author of *It came upon the midnight clear,* the US pastor and writer Edmund Hamilton Sears (1810-1876), was a minister in a Church which does not subscribe to the doctrine of the Trinity, and that the hymn has been condemned as not really a hymn at all. The hymn scholar Erik Routley wrote that 'in its original form, the hymn is little more than an ethical song, extolling the worth and splendour of peace among men'.

It is true that the hymn does not in fact mention God or the Lord Jesus Christ, and that Sears was a Unitarian minister, but there is more to him than meets the eye.

He was theologically very conservative by Unitarian standards, believing in a fully human and fully divine Christ. He was deeply interested in the mystical tradition, and had a theologically independent mind which sometimes took him off in odd directions. A passionate opponent of slavery, he forecast before the Civil War that America would 'reap the whirlwind' of its sin.

The hymn, written in 1849, arose from a period of illness and depression which resulted in him leaving a large and successful ministry and returning to his first countryside church, where he had been very happy. Its references to the 'Babel sounds' of human strife, 'man at war with man' and the 'men of strife' are very topical. Not only did he fear for the future of his own nation, but Europe had just suffered its 'Year of Revolutions' in which governments across the continent had been swept violently from power. 1848 saw the publication of the *Communist Manifesto*, and the United States had just fought a war with Mexico regarded by many – including the recently-elected congressman Abraham Lincoln – as an unjustifiable attempt at a land-grab.

It is possible to read *It came upon the midnight clear* as a humanist hymn, but that does not really do justice either to its author or to the hymn itself. Sears was a devout Christian who was deeply troubled by the state of the world around him and he wrote the hymn to express God's desire for peace through the rule of the Prince of Peace. The last verse mixes Greek thinking – the prophet-bards and the age of gold – with biblical imagery, but his heart is in the right place.

For orthodox Christians, human efforts to make a perfect world can only be completed by the gracious act of God, who in the end will make all things new. Sears seems to have this in mind in the last verse; if not, it is certainly how we should sing it.

In a world which is even more troubled today than it was in 1849, and when our fears are greater, this is a hymn to be sung with understanding. More than a musical Christmas decoration, it has something profoundly important to say.

My song is love unknown,
My Saviour's love to me;
Love to the loveless shown,
That they might lovely be.
O who am I,
That for my sake
My Lord should take
Frail flesh, and die?

He came from his blest throne
Salvation to bestow;
But men made strange, and none
The longed-for Christ would know:
But oh, my Friend,
My Friend indeed,
Who at my need
His life did spend.

Sometimes they strew his way,
And his sweet praises sing;
Resounding all the day
Hosannas to their King:
Then 'Crucify!'
Is all their breath,
And for his death
They thirst and cry.

Why, what hath my Lord done?
What makes this rage and spite?
He made the lame to run,
He gave the blind their sight,
Sweet injuries!
Yet they at these
Themselves displease,
and 'gainst him rise,

*They rise and needs will have
My dear Lord made away;
A murderer they save,
The Prince of life they slay.
Yet cheerful he
To suffering goes,
That he his foes
From thence might free.*

*In life, no house, no home
My Lord on earth might have;
In death, no friendly tomb,
But what a stranger gave.
What may I say?
Heav'n was his home;
But mine the tomb
Wherein he lay.*

*Here might I stay and sing,
No story so divine;
Never was love, dear King,
Never was grief like thine.
This is my Friend,
In whose sweet praise
I all my days
Could gladly spend.*

My song is love unknown

IT is very rare that a hymn of such length, with a tune that is slow, thoughtful and meditative, survives uncut in the frenetic atmosphere that characterises both the modern world and, all too often, the modern service of worship. *My song is love unknown* is not shortened, though. It has an integrity which makes one verse follow another seamlessly and a tone of quiet grief which would make it almost a sacrilege to omit any of it.

It was written by Samuel Crossman and published in 1664 in *The Young Man's Meditation, or Some Few Sacred Poems upon Select Subjects, and Scriptures*. The title is not very promising, but this hymn is one of the few from the time that are still worth singing. It is simple, direct but profoundly felt, avoiding as it does the forced poetical style and theological aggressiveness that characterised too much of what was produced in those days.

Its dominant theme is the contradiction between who Christ was and what was done to him. Each verse develops a different aspect of this. There is 'love to the loveless shown'. He came to bestow salvation, but 'men made strange'; the gift was spurned. The people themselves are inconsistent, strewing palm branches before him and singing his praises one minute and calling for his death the next. Yet all his actions were good; 'He made the lame to run, he gave the blind their sight'. In spite of this, 'A murderer they saved, the Prince of life they slay'.

The hymn arguably comes to a point in the lines: 'What may I say? Heav'n was his home; but mine the tomb wherein he lay.' Christ suffered the death to which we are all destined because of our sinful nature, but freely and willingly; he endured the causeless 'rage and spite' of his enemies for our sakes.

Crossman was an Anglican clergyman of the Puritan wing. Puritans have had a bad press over the years, but they were sincere, learned, faithful and many of them were much more fun than people assume. Crossman had the misfortune to live in a time of great change and religious tension. Oliver Cromwell's Church was Presbyterian and Puritan, but when Charles II resumed the throne the religious and theological confusions of the time – with a constant threat of religiously-motivated violence – were felt to have got out of hand. A conference to try to resolve them and create a state Church which would include Puritans failed, and in 1662 the Act of Uniformity was passed. Clergy who could not agree to its Prayer Book theology were excluded, and around 2,000 of the best and brightest Anglican ministers resigned. It was an event which many regarded as a catastrophe, leading to the spiritual drought of the 18th century.

Crossman was one of them. However, he soon changed his mind and returned to the Anglican fold; life was very hard for those excluded, who often had no means of support. He became a royal chaplain and then Dean of Bristol Cathedral.

This hymn speaks powerfully, and sadly, of human weakness and inconsistency; perhaps Crossman recognised, and regretted, his own.

Now thank we all our God,
With heart and hands and voices,
Who wondrous things has done,
In whom his world rejoices;
Who from our mothers' arms
Has blessed us on our way
With countless gifts of love,
And still is ours today.

O may this bounteous God
Through all our life be near us,
With ever joyful hearts
And blessèd peace to cheer us;
And keep us in his grace,
And guide us when perplexed;
And free us from all ills,
In this world and the next.

All praise and thanks to God
The Father now be given;
The Son and him who reigns
With them in highest heaven;
The one eternal God,
Whom earth and heaven adore;
For thus it was, is now,
And shall be evermore.

Now thank we all our God

THE Thirty Years War was one of the most destructive in European history. From 1618-1648 a bitter, confused and savage conflict raged, with consequences for the states which were to become Germany which were even worse than those of the First and Second World Wars. Up to 30 per cent of the population died, while in some areas the loss was as much as 75 per cent. Religion was one of the reasons, with Catholics and Protestants at each others' throats, but power and land were just as important.

Martin Rinkart was a Lutheran pastor in Eilenburg in Saxony, and saw some of the worst of the fighting. Towards the end of the war, his city was flooded with refugees, 800 homes were destroyed, and famine and plague carried off thousands. The pastors died too, and Rinkart found himself conducting 50 funerals a day. The besieging Swedish army demanded a huge ransom to leave the city alone, and Rinkart bravely went to plead with them for mercy; impressed by his courage, they withdrew.

The people of Eilenburg held a grand celebration, and Rinkart composed the hymn *Now thank we all our God*.

It became known to English-speaking Christians thanks to its translation by Catherine Winkworth in 1856 – many great German hymns found their way into our hymn books thanks to her. It is remarkable for its serene faith and absolute confidence in the goodness of God. In spite of the horrors he had seen, Rinkart was able to write of the 'wondrous things' God has done, and the 'countless gifts of love' which he has given to his people. God is 'bounteous', he blesses us with peace and joyful hearts, and keeps us now and in eternity.

Understanding the background to the hymn helps us to sing it as more than just a bland statement of theological principles, or a shallow devotional formula. Rinkart had seen far worse than we shall ever see, but came through his experiences with his faith intact and with a deep conviction of the love of God.

To be able to thank God in spite of the bad times we go through is often difficult, and it might look to people who do not share our faith like foolishness. But someone has said, 'Never doubt in the darkness what God has shown you in the light.' This is a hymn which looks the world in the face, and still dares to thank God for his goodness.

Now the green blade riseth, from the buried grain,
Wheat that in the dark earth many days has lain;
Love lives again, that with the dead has been:
Love is come again, like wheat that springeth green.

Now the green blade riseth

SOME of the great Easter hymns we sing are hundreds of years old, with deep roots in Church tradition. Old does not necessarily mean good, but hymns which still speak after so many years have to have something about them.

A more modern classic is *Now the green blade riseth*, by J M C Crum (1872-1958). First published in 1928, its haunting melody (the late 15th century *Noel Nouvelet*) is combined with powerful and persuasive imagery. It is not a comfortable or particularly easy hymn to sing well, but it speaks to our hearts – and will probably still be speaking many years from now, like the ancient Easter hymns of our spiritual ancestors.

The idea is simple enough, and comes from John 12. 24: 'I tell you the truth, unless a kernel of wheat falls to the ground and dies, it remains only a single seed. But if it dies, it produces many seeds' (NIV). It is not a precise match, but that is the germ of the idea. The seed is dead, to all appearance; it is buried, as we might bury a corpse – but miraculously, come the spring, the green blade appears and new life begins. Christ was dead, he was buried, and on the third day he rose again.

The hymn is written with a deep sense of wonder at the power of God in creation, and considerable skill. 'Now the green blade riseth from the buried grain,/ Wheat that in dark earth many days has lain': we see the contrasting colours, the green of the blade, the black winter earth, and though most of us are city-dwellers now we still respond to the sense of spring after winter.

But it is not polished Victorian versifying, either, though Crum was well-schooled in that form. He makes us work to fit the tune to the words: 'Thinking that never he would wake again' and 'He that for three days in the grave had lain' do not flow naturally. There is a deliberate awkwardness which fits the mood of the hymn. If it were easier it would not be as memorable.

Like all great hymns, it moves from the truths of scripture to the truths of human nature in relationship with God. Its refrain is, 'Love is come again, like wheat that springeth green'. The last verse makes the connection explicit:

> *When our hearts are wintry, grieving, or in pain,*
> *Thy touch can call us back to life again;*
> *Fields of our hearts that dead and bare have been ...*

This is very powerful writing, which leaves us, whenever we look out over a personal wasteland, with the gift of hope.

John MacLeod Campbell Crum was of course of Scottish ancestry, though born in Cheshire. He was an Anglican clergyman, a scholar, poet and pastor, with a particular ministry to children. He had several respectable appointments – chaplain to the Bishop of Oxford and assistant curate of Windsor, for instance, and finished his career as a Canon of Canterbury – but his first curacy at Darlington made him a life-long socialist.

He wrote a good deal, but this hymn is the one for which he is remembered.

O come, O come, Emmanuel,
And ransom captive Israel,
That mourns in lonely exile here
Until the Son of God appear.

    Rejoice! Rejoice!
    Emmanuel shall come to thee, O Israel.

O come, thou Wisdom from on high,
Who orderest all things mightily;
To us the path of knowledge show,
And teach us in her ways to go.

O come, thou Rod of Jesse, free
Thine own from Satan's tyranny;
From depths of hell thy people save,
And give them victory over the grave.

O come, thou Day-spring, come and cheer
Our spirits by thine advent here;
Disperse the gloomy clouds of night,
And death's dark shadows put to flight.

O come, thou Key of David, come,
And open wide our heavenly home;
Make safe the way that leads on high,
And close the path to misery.

O come, O come, great Lord of might,
Who to thy tribes on Sinai's height
In ancient times didst give the law
In cloud and majesty and awe.

O come, Desire of nations, bind
In one the hearts of all mankind;
And bid our sad divisions cease,
And be thyself our King of Peace.

O come, O come Immanuel

O COME, O come Immanuel is one of those very great hymns which is in danger of passing out of use, at least in the evangelical Protestant tradition. Its tune, *Veni Emmanuel,* drawn from a 15th century processional of French Franciscan nuns. This has a mournful tone at odds with the chorus, which tells us to 'rejoice, rejoice'.

The original Latin words date from the 12th century, and they were translated by the noted hymn-writer John Mason Neale, who rescued many ancient texts and brought them back into the living worship of the Church.

The verses each take a biblical description of Christ (except the second, where the 'Lord of Might' is God the Father) and take it as a theme for prayer. The rod of Jesse (Isaiah 11. 1) stands for power and authority – so, 'From depths of hell thy people save.'

The dayspring, or dawn, is from Zechariah's words in Luke 1. 78; spiritually, Christ will 'disperse the gloomy clouds of night,' and put death's shadow to flight. The key of David is in Isaiah 22. 22; Christ will 'open wide our heavenly home'.

These are not references which spring easily to mind, but they are very thought-provoking, and arise from a deep knowledge of the scripture. There has been a wonderful expansion of song-writing in different styles over the last few years, and there is no doubt that the simple directness of many of them speaks powerfully to parts of us that classical hymns could not reach. However, they suffer sometimes from their simplicity; they do not give us very much to think about, and in the end, if they are our only diet, our worship is impoverished. This is one of those hymns which gives us more to think about every time we sing it.

It is ideal for Advent, speaking as it does about the coming Messiah. However, it can also be very creatively used at other times of the year, perhaps during a serious time of intercession. The verses do not have to be sung in a vacuum; each of them can be related to the real experience of God's people today. We are in exile, as the first verse says; God is mighty to save (verse 2); Christians are sometimes oppressed, and need help (verse 3); we fail and are downhearted (verse 4); we have a home in heaven, and a glorious hope (verse 5).

It is a lovely hymn, and very rich in meaning. It would be a pity if we were to lose the habit of singing it: it does us good to grapple with hard things from time to time.

There are various versions of the lyrics, and not all the verses are nowadays sung.

O dearest Lord, thy sacred head
With thorns was pierced for me;
O pour thy blessing on my head
That I may think for thee.

O, dearest Lord, thy sacred head

AN almost-forgotten clergyman hero of the Anglo-Catholic revival was responsible for a very beautiful hymn, which can be sung at Communion services or as a dedication song after a sermon.

Henry Ernest Hardy (1869-1946), known for most of his life as Father Andrew, was the author *O dearest Lord, thy sacred head,* whose deceptively simple but technically accomplished verses are an extended meditation on the wounds of Christ.

His head, hands, feet and heart were pierced with thorns, nails and spear. So, Father Andrew prays, 'O pour thy blessing on my head/ That I may think for thee' – and work, follow and live for thee.

The hymn is not remarkable for any vivid or striking imagery. It is brief, only four verses, and it does not develop a theme. It simply focuses on Christ, and invites us to think of his sufferings and echo them in the offering of our lives in his service. It does not force us to make connections with the gritty realities of life, and it would be easy to dismiss it as a piece of Victorian piety divorced from reality.

However, this is one of those hymns where knowing something about the life of its author can help intensify the effect of the verse. Henry Hardy was born in India, the son of an Indian Army colonel who had helped put down the Mutiny. He was academically undistinguished; Clifton College in Bristol and Keble College, Oxford, only resulted in a fourth-class degree. But he came under the influence of Arthur Winnington-Ingram, later Bishop of London, who visited the University in search of volunteers to work with the poor in London. Winnington-Ingram's reputation was tarnished for later generations by his anti-German rhetoric during the Great War, but in his effect on Hardy, at least, his words bore a more worthy fruit. Hardy moved to Oxford House in the East End in 1891.

In 1894, with James Adderley and Henry Chappel, he founded the Society of Divine Compassion, taking vows of poverty, chastity and obedience. He was the mainstay of the community, and its last survivor – Adderley left in 1897 and Chappel died in 1915. It was based in Plaistow, where Hardy was priest-in-charge of St Philip's church from 1916 until his death.

He was a talented artist and writer as well as a social activist, writing passion plays which his friend Lilian Bayliss staged at the Old Vic. A dedicated priest, his letters, published immediately after his death, became a spiritual classic. He was described by one bishop as 'a great man, such as God sends only once or twice in a generation'. His death from cancer was accelerated by the strains he endured as the East End was bombed during the war.

So *O dearest Lord* is rooted in a deep commitment to the poor, and is the testament of a faithful servant of Christ whose life mirrored his words.

O God of Bethel, by whose hand
Thy people still are fed;
Who through this earthly pilgrimage
Hast all our fathers led:

Our vows, our prayers, we now present
Before thy throne of grace:
God of our fathers, be the God
Of their succeeding race.

Through each perplexing path of life
Our wandering footsteps guide;
Give us each day our daily bread,
And raiment fit provide.

O spread thy covering wings around,
Till all our wanderings cease,
And at our Father's loved abode
Our souls arrive in peace!

Such blessings from thy gracious hand
Our humble prayers implore;
And thou shalt be our covenant God
And portion evermore.

O God of Bethel

THERE are many hymns that ask for God's blessing and protection on his pilgrim people. The story of the Exodus and the wandering in the wilderness that followed has always seemed a fitting metaphor for the life of God's people today. We are lost, we do wander, but we do sense that we are not abandoned and that God is with us wherever we go.

Philip Doddridge (1702-1751) was the author of *O God of Bethel, by whose hand*.

He was a Nonconformist minister in Northampton, the founder of a Dissenting Academy (Nonconformists were not allowed to graduate from Oxford or Cambridge and had to attend their own colleges) and a prolific hymn writer. His reputation as a preacher, scholar and pastor was huge, and he was admired across denominational boundaries: his book *The Rise and Progress of Religion in the Soul* had the effect of converting William Wilberforce, the great anti-slavery campaigner, and was later described by C H Spurgeon as 'that holy book'. He died of tuberculosis, having been weakened by overwork.

O God of Bethel, like many of his 400 hymns, was written to illustrate a sermon. He was not the only minister of his age to do this; in the 18th and 19th centuries verse-writing was taught, and it would occur more naturally to educated pastors that they might drive home their lessons in that way. Of course many of them were dry and mechanical exercises, and many of Doddridge's own have not survived in use. *O God of Bethel*, however, has a beautiful simplicity about it that means it will be singable for many years to come.

It harks back to the Exodus, and the 'weary pilgrimage' of God's people through the years of wilderness wandering. But it is above all an expression of faith. It takes the faithfulness of God during the Exodus years as a pattern of his faithfulness today. He kept his people then, and he will keep us now: 'God of our fathers, be the God/ Of their succeeding race.'

The verse is simple and straightforward, using plain English words rather than the elaborate Latinate ones favoured by many poets of the time – count the number of monosyllables.

However, simple does not mean simplistic. Doddridge was soaked in scripture, and he expected his congregation to be as well. When he wrote 'Through each perplexing path of life/ Our wandering footsteps guide' he would have expected them to remember the pillar of cloud which led the people by day and the pillar of fire which led them by night. When he wrote 'Give us each day our daily bread,/And raiment fit provide' he was referring to the manna which fell from heaven, and the verse in Deuteronomy 29. 5 in which Moses says: 'I have led you forty years in the wilderness. Your clothes have not worn out on you, and your sandals have not worn off your feet.'

In the last verse, which begins 'O spread thy covering wings around', we move to the Psalms: 'He will cover you with his pinions, and under his wings you will find refuge' (Psalm 91.4).

From a scriptural point of view, though, the most interesting reference is in the first verse, to the 'God of Bethel'. This is where Jacob fell asleep and dreamed of a ladder reaching up to heaven, and received God's promise that he would be the father of a great nation. All the wanderings of God's people are in the light of that promise and that vision. The 'God of Bethel' has made even greater promises to us.

The hymn was sung at the Queen's Silver Jubilee in 1977. Since then she and her family have known good times and bad, but they have always known God's saving and keeping power.

O little town of Bethlehem,
   How still we see thee lie!
Above thy deep and dreamless sleep
The silent stars go by.
Yet in thy dark streets shineth
The everlasting light;
The hopes and fears of all the years
Are met in thee tonight.

For Christ is born of Mary,
And gathered all above,
While mortals sleep, the angels keep
Their watch of wondering love.
O morning stars together,
Proclaim the holy birth,
And praises sing to God the King,
And peace to men on earth!

How silently, how silently,
The wondrous gift is giv'n;
So God imparts to human hearts
The blessings of his heav'n.
No ear may hear his coming,
But in this world of sin,
Where meek souls will receive him, still
The dear Christ enters in.

O holy child of Bethlehem,
Descend to us, we pray;
Cast out our sin, and enter in,
Be born in us today.
We hear the Christmas angels
The great glad tidings tell;
O come to us, abide with us,
Our Lord Emmanuel!

O little town of Bethlehem

PHILLIPS Brooks (1835-93) was a hugely influential American Episcopalian (Anglican) clergyman and teacher. He was rector of Trinity Church in Boston, Massachusetts, which he rebuilt in a grand style as one of the ecclesiastical wonders of the Eastern United States, and briefly served as Bishop of Massachusetts. Physically imposing at 6ft 4ins, he was a renowned preacher and his lectures on preaching are still read today.

He was also a passionate opponent of slavery during the dark years of the American Civil War and campaigned for freed slaves to be able to vote. When he died, according to one observer, 'They buried him like a king. Harvard students carried his body on their shoulders. All barriers of denomination were down. Roman Catholics and Unitarians felt that a great man had fallen in Israel.'

With all his achievements in his native country, he is best remembered today for the hymn he wrote after a visit to the Holy Land. On Christmas Eve 1865 he went to a midnight service at the Church of the Holy Nativity in Bethlehem, and wrote: 'I remember standing in the old church in Bethlehem, close to the spot where Jesus was born, when the whole church was ringing hour after hour with splendid hymns of praise to God, how again and again it seemed as if I could hear voices I knew well, telling each other of the Wonderful Night of the Saviour's birth.'

Two years later he wrote *O Little Town of Bethlehem*, one of the best-known of all carols. It is a remarkably vivid picture of the actual city (and in that pre-electric age the streets would indeed have been 'dark', and the stillness would have been much deeper than it ever would be today). But the hymn takes the place he knew, and peoples it with the characters of the Christmas story: here is Christ born of Mary, and the angels keeping their watch of wondering love. It is also full of theology, not in a heavy-handed statement of doctrine, but in a preacher's interpretation of what the doctrine really means in the life of the believer:

> *'How silently, how silently,*
> *The wondrous Gift is giv'n;*
> *So God imparts to human hearts*
> *The blessings of his heav'n.'*

Salvation Songs

There is a deep feeling and poetic vision in these verses, arising from a profound engagement with the events they describe. The theme which runs through them is that Christmas is not just a single historical event: it is God breaking in to the world, which happens not just when his Son is incarnate, but when his will is done. A verse which is not generally found in our hymnbooks today runs:

> *Where children pure and happy*
> *Pray to the blessèd Child,*
> *Where misery cries out to thee,*
> *Son of the mother mild;*
> *Where charity stands watching*
> *And faith holds wide the door,*
> *The dark night wakes, the glory breaks,*
> *And Christmas comes once more.*

We are more familiar with the lines which run:

> *No ear may hear his coming,*
> *But in this world of sin,*
> *Where meek souls will receive him, still*
> *The dear Christ enters in.*

We know, too, the last verse which has the line, 'Cast out our sin, and enter in, be born in us today.'

There is a profound truth here, that Christ comes into the world in and through us disciples, as well as in Bethlehem 2,000 years ago.

O love of God, how strong and true!
Eternal, and yet ever new;
Uncomprehended and unbought,
Beyond all knowledge and all thought.

O heavenly love, how precious still,
In days of weariness and ill,
In nights of pain and helplessness,
To heal, to comfort, and to bless!

O wide embracing, wondrous love!
We read thee in the sky above,
We read thee in the earth below,
In seas that swell, and streams that flow.

We read thee best in him who came
To bear for us the cross of shame;
Sent by the Father from on high,
Our life to live, our death to die.

We read thy power to bless and save,
E'en in the darkness of the grave;
Still more in resurrection light,
We read the fullness of thy might.

O love of God, our shield and stay
Through all the perils of our way!
Eternal love, in thee we rest
Forever safe, forever blest.

O Love of God, how strong and true

HORATIUS Bonar has been called 'the prince of Scottish hymn writers'. He was born and died in Edinburgh (1808-1889), his long life spanning the rise and high water mark of Evangelicalism in the UK. Several of his hymns – he wrote more than 600 – are still sung today, and *O love of God, how strong and true* is well known and loved. Among other claims to fame, it was sung at the funeral of US president Ronald Reagan.

One reason for its popularity is that it is deeply theological, while being free of the sort of sectarian dogmatising which wrecked a good number of otherwise good hymns of the period. Bonar was not a shrinking violet in his personal convictions: he was one of a number of clergymen to leave the Church of Scotland on the grounds of conscience after the Disruption of 1843. But *O love of God* can be sung by any Christian, of whatever persuasion.

On the face of it, it ought to be easy to write about the love of God. We all believe in it, and the Bible gives us many examples of it. But it is not as straightforward as that. We need some flesh on the bones. What does the love of God look like? What does it mean? What difference does it make in our lives, and why should we believe it?

A song about love can easily degenerate into mere emotionalism. Some hymns and worship songs do just that, unfortunately. They do not survive long, as they have nothing to teach us and we are soon bored by them. We need songs that match our growing Christian experience, and that reflect how we struggle to do the right thing when we are tempted, or struggle to live hopefully when life seems to be against us. In a way, it is like the stages of love: it might begin with a passionate devotion, when we are consumed by desire, but it matures into something far richer and deeper. Often couples who have been married a long time will say that they love each other far more after the passage of the years, because they have found more to love.

Bonar's hymn arises from great spiritual maturity. He has thought and prayed long and hard about the love of God and so he can bring us a three-dimensional image of it. He begins with a statement about its nature which is almost mystical in its intensity: it is 'Eternal, and yet ever new;/ Uncomprehended and unbought,/Beyond all knowledge and all thought.'

But we know its reality too, 'In days of weariness and ill', when it heals, comforts and blesses, and 'In nights of pain and helplessness' (there speaks the pastor who has watched by the beds of the dying). We see it in the natural world, in the sky above and the earth below. Most of all, we see it in Jesus, particularly in his death on the cross for us.

But that is not the climax of the hymn: God's love is there 'E'en in the darkness of the grave' and 'Still more in resurrection light.' These are separate ideas. It is not that resurrection, the power of God even over death, is what brings death within the circle of God's love; even death itself is under his control, and we are not forsaken in it. God, says Horatius Bonar, is Lord of All.

*O Love that wilt not let me go,
 I rest my weary soul in thee;
I give thee back the life I owe,
That in thine ocean depths its flow
May richer, fuller be.*

*O light that followest all my way,
I yield my flickering torch to thee;
My heart restores its borrowed ray,
That in thy sunshine's blaze its day
May brighter, fairer be.*

*O joy that seekest me through pain,
I cannot close my heart to thee;
I trace the rainbow through the rain,
And feel the promise is not vain,
That morn shall tearless be.*

*O cross that liftest up my head,
I dare not ask to fly from thee;
I lay in dust life's glory dead,
And from the ground there blossoms red
Life that shall endless be.*

O Love that wilt not let me go

SOME hymns are beyond criticism, and *O Love that wilt not let me go* is one. It is beautiful devotional verse, in which the author, the blind hymn-writer George Matheson, takes different facets of the Christian life and turns them into metaphors for God's dealings with us. Each one is developed with great wisdom and insight, the fruit of Matheson's own prayers and reading (he was a considerable scholar, thanks in part to the care of his elder sister, who read to him). He was also an experienced Church of Scotland pastor and preacher, with an astonishing memory – he could quote whole passages of scripture by heart, and many of his hearers did not realise he was blind.

It is rare that we know the date of a hymn so exactly, but he has left us a record.

'My hymn was composed in the manse of Innelan [Argyleshire, Scotland] on the evening of the 6th of June, 1882, when I was 40 years of age,' he says. 'I was alone in the manse at that time. It was the night of my sister's marriage, and the rest of the family were staying overnight in Glasgow.

'Something happened to me, which was known only to myself, and which caused me the most severe mental suffering. The hymn was the fruit of that suffering.

'It was the quickest bit of work I ever did in my life. I had the impression of having it dictated to me by some inward voice rather than of working it out myself. I am quite sure that the whole work was completed in five minutes, and equally sure that it never received at my hands any retouching or correction. I have no natural gift of rhythm. All the other verses I have ever written are manufactured articles; this came like a dayspring from on high.'

There has always been speculation about the occasion of the hymn. One suggestion is that a fiancée broke their engagement when she learned that he was going blind. There is more romance than reality about this, though, because Matheson was almost completely blind from the age of about 20. We shall probably never know.

In the hymn, he writes of the love that will not let us go, the light that follows all our way, the joy that seeks us through pain, and – most movingly of all – the 'Cross that liftest up my head'. That line refers to Christ being lifted up in crucifixion, and perhaps what follows, 'I dare not ask to fly from thee,' reflect his own acceptance of the limitations he suffered. Nevertheless, it ends, 'I lay in dust life's glory dead,/ And from the ground there blossoms red/ Life that shall endless be.'

Whatever the trial which gave rise to the hymn, this note of faith was typical of him. He once wrote of his life that it was 'an obstructed life, a circumscribed life ... but a life of quenchless hopefulness, a life which has beaten persistently against the cage of circumstance, and which even at the time of abandoned work has said not "Good night" but "Good morning."'

Matheson said that he wrote the hymn in five minutes, but it was the fruit of a lifetime's walk with God. When he says he felt it was 'dictated by some inward voice' we have no reason to doubt him. It is the distillation of all he had learned and felt and believed.

It is usually sung to *St Margaret*, by Albert Lister Peace (1844-1912), a gifted organist and composer.

O *sacred head, sore wounded,*
 With grief and shame weighed down;
How scornfully surrounded
With thorns, thine only crown;
How pale art thou with anguish,
With sore abuse and scorn;
How does that visage languish,
Which once was bright as morn!

What thou, my Lord, hast suffered
Was all for sinners' gain:
Mine, mine was the transgression,
But thine the deadly pain.
Lo, here I fall, my Saviour!
'Tis I deserve thy place;
Look on me with thy favour,
Vouchsafe to me thy grace.

What language shall I borrow
To thank thee, dearest friend,
For this thy dying sorrow,
Thy pity without end?
O make me thine for ever;
And should I fainting be,
Lord, let me never, never
Outlive my love to thee.

Be near when I'm dying,
O show thy cross to me;
And for my succour flying,
Come, Lord, to set me free:
These eyes, new faith receiving,
From Jesus shall not move;
And he who dies believing,
Dies safely, through thy love.

O sacred head, sore wounded

THE crucifixion of the Lord Jesus Christ is part of the central drama of the Christian faith, but there are surprisingly few hymns which focus unflinchingly on that event and its meaning. Perhaps we prefer the warm and easy shallows of faith to its dangerous depths.

One hymn which does bring us face to face with the deepest mysteries of the faith is *O sacred head, sore wounded*.

It has a long history. The English versions we sing are based on mediaeval Latin poem by Arnulf of Louvain (d.1250), though for a long time it was thought that Bernard of Clairvaux – described by the Reformer Martin Luther as 'the best monk that ever lived' – was the author. The poem, *Salve mundi salutare*, addresses the different parts of Christ's body on the cross, like the purely English hymn *O dearest Lord, thy sacred head*; our English hymn is taken from the last part.

Salve caput cruentatum has been translated into English several times, notably by Robert Bridges and Ronald Knox. Most of us sing a variant of a version by James Waddel Alexander (1804-1859). He was a Presbyterian minister and scholar from Virginia, and his version was much longer than the four or five verses we know today; editors have improved it over the years.

The words are moving just as verse, but matched with J S Bach's beautiful *Passion Chorale* the hymn becomes a profoundly spiritual experience. It does not wallow in blood and gore like Mel Gibson's film *The Passion of the Christ*, but it is clear about Christ's physical suffering, the 'sore abuse and scorn' he went through, with thorns his only crown. The intimately personal nature of salvation is brought out in the second verse:

> *What thou, my Lord, hast suffered*
> *Was all for sinners' gain;*
> *Mine, mine was the transgression,*
> *But thine the deadly pain.*

'All we like sheep have gone astray,' says Isaiah; 'we have turned – every one – to his own way; and the Lord has laid on him the iniquity of us all' (Isaiah 53. 6).

This 'dying sorrow, thy pity without end' calls out a response in us, of lifelong gratitude and love – 'Lord, let me never, never/ Outlive my love to thee.'

But it is not our love for Jesus which keeps us at the end; when we face death it is God himself who preserves us in faith, and 'they who die believing/ Die safely through thy love.'

This hymn is one of the treasures of the Church. If we spend time with it and let it speak to us, it will lead us to a greater love for Christ, and a deeper understanding of his love that passes knowledge.

O worship the King, all glorious above,
O gratefully sing his power and his love;
Our shield and defender, the Ancient of Days,
Pavilioned in splendour, and girded with praise.

O tell of his might, O sing of his grace,
Whose robe is the light, whose canopy space.
His chariots of wrath the deep thunderclouds form,
And dark is his path on the wings of the storm.

The earth with its store of wonders untold,
Almighty, thy power hath founded of old;
Established it fast by a changeless decree,
And round it hath cast, like a mantle, the sea.

Thy bountiful care, what tongue can recite?
It breathes in the air, it shines in the light;
It streams from the hills, it descends to the plain,
And sweetly distills in the dew and the rain.

Frail children of dust, and feeble as frail,
In thee do we trust, nor find thee to fail;
Thy mercies how tender, how firm to the end,
Our maker, defender, redeemer and friend.

O measureless might! Ineffable love!
While angels delight to hymn thee above,
The humbler creation, though feeble their lays,
With true adoration shall sing to thy praise.

O worship the King

ONE OF the great Christian hymns, sung with gusto in every Christian tradition, is *O worship the King*. Written by Robert Grant (1779-1838), it is a glorious shout of praise to God, strengthened even more when it is sung to the majestic *Hanover* by William Croft (so named in honour of the Hanoverian kings who followed the House of Stuart on the British throne).

But it is more than just a series of slogans. It is a thoughtful and very skilful reflection on God as the Creator and Sustainer of life. It moves from considering the grand scale of the physical creation to acknowledging God's care for each one of his children.

The King is 'all-glorious above', 'pavilioned in splendour, the ancient of days' – the imagery is drawn from Daniel 7. The hymn comes closer than any other to expressing the awe-inspiring majesty of God. But it also speaks of God's 'bountiful care,' which 'breathes in the air' and 'shines in the light'; God, for Grant, is not distant and unknowable; he is intimately involved with human beings, and blesses all of us throughout our lives. We are 'Frail children of dust, and feeble as frail,' but 'In thee do we trust, nor find thee to fail.'

But it is the majesty of God which is the theme of this hymn, and it draws its imagery from the majesty of nature.

Robert Grant was a successful lawyer and administrator who was born in Bengal (his father was a director of the East India Company). He moved back to Scotland with his family when he was only six, and in time became a dedicated and reforming member of Parliament (he was responsible for the emancipation of Britain's Jews). He was a sponsor of evangelical causes throughout his life.

He returned to India as Governor of Bombay in 1834, dying only four years later.

It may be that in writing the second verse, which contains the thrilling lines 'His chariots of wrath/ The deep thunder clouds form/ And dark is his path/ On the wings of the storm' he was thinking not of Britain's milder climate, but of the onrush of the Indian monsoon, when nature's power is seen in its full strength – and is still subject to the will of God, who can calm the storm with a word.

Interestingly, the hymn is not entirely original. It was based on one by William Kethe (?-1594) who was one of the translators of the Geneva Bible and wrote *All people that on earth do dwell*. One of Kethe's verses read, 'His chamber beams lie, in the clouds full sure,/ Which as his chariot, are made him to bear/ And there with much swiftness his course doth endure:/ Upon the wings riding, of winds in the air.'

*Peace, perfect peace, in this dark world of sin?
The blood of Jesus whispers peace within.*

*Peace, perfect peace, by thronging duties pressed?
To do the will of Jesus, this is rest.*

*Peace, perfect peace, with sorrows surging round?
On Jesus' bosom naught but calm is found.*

*Peace, perfect peace, with loved ones far away?
In Jesus' keeping we are safe, and they.*

*Peace, perfect peace, our future all unknown?
Jesus we know, and he is on the throne.*

*Peace, perfect peace, death shadowing us and ours?
Jesus has vanquished death and all its powers.*

*It is enough: earth's struggles soon shall cease,
And Jesus call us to heaven's perfect peace.*

Peace, perfect peace

MANY of us live lives that are far too busy. We rush from work to home and back, with not enough time to be quiet and think, or pray, or just spend quality time with people we love. There's too much going on, and we feel guilty about not achieving something every day.

Or perhaps we are overwhelmed not by business, but by circumstances beyond our control – illness, or sorrow, or some kind of failure. How, we wonder, can we find peace?

Edward Henry Bickersteth (1825-1905) wrote *Peace, perfect peace* in 1875, at the height of the Victorian era – now distant in time, but not so far in terms of human nature and the trials and tribulations which we still face today.

He was Dean of Gloucester and then Bishop of Exeter, but he was first and foremost a pastor. He wrote the hymn on holiday in Harrogate, after hearing a sermon on Isaiah 26. 3, 'Thou wilt keep him in perfect peace, whose mind is stayed on thee' (AV). In Hebrew, the preacher said, what is translated as 'perfect peace' is the word for 'peace' repeated – 'peace, peace' – to express perfection.

That afternoon he had to visit a dying relative, and read Isaiah's words to him; then he wrote down the hymn just as we have it now, and read it to him.

It is a beautiful expression of profound faith and trust in God, whatever the circumstances of life might be. Its simplicity masks the skilfulness of the verse. It is a series of questions and answers, each question expressing a real dilemma for Christians today. How can there be perfect peace in this world of sin, when we are oppressed by 'thronging duties', when sorrows surge round, when we are far from those we love, fearful of the future, living every day in the knowledge that we will one day die?

These are deep questions, which we are not always comfortable asking. Indeed, what sometimes looks like the frantic pursuit of entertainment and information through ever-greater connectedness via social networking and news websites might be at least in part an attempt to avoid facing up to our own mortality. Bickersteth offers no easy answers; he simply points us to Jesus and invites us to look for hope in him.

It is sung to *Pax Tecum* ('peace be with you'). This tune, with its first line of repeated notes, can drag if it is not played sensitively and at a reasonable speed. But as the melody enters in the second line, it is very well adapted to the sense of the verses; an opening tension, with a satisfying resolution for each one.

Ride on, ride on, in majesty!
Hark! all the tribes 'Hosanna' cry;
Thy humble beast pursues his road
With palms and scattered garments strowed.

Ride on, ride on, in majesty!
In lowly pomp ride on to die!
O Christ! Thy triumphs now begin
O'er captive death and conquered sin.

Ride on, ride on, in majesty!
The wingèd squadrons of the skies
Look down with sad and wondering eyes
To see the approaching sacrifice.

Ride on, ride on, in majesty!
Thy last and fiercest strife is nigh;
The Father, on his sapphire throne,
Expects his own anointed Son.

Ride on, ride on, in majesty!
In lowly pomp ride on to die;
Bow thy meek head to mortal pain,
Then take, O God, thy power, and reign.

Ride on, ride on in majesty

THE last days of Jesus before his crucifixion are rich with stories, and one of them which seems to have a great depth of meaning is that of the triumphal entry into Jerusalem. Many hymn-writers have dealt with it at many different levels – including Fred Kaan, who wrote, perhaps unwisely, *We have a King who rides a donkey* to the tune of *What shall we do with a drunken sailor?*

But there is far more to the story than this, and *Ride on, ride on* in majesty captures not just the irony and pathos of the event, but explores its theology as well.

Jesus is welcomed as a king entering his capital city, but riding on a donkey, a non-threatening symbol of peace, rather than on a charger. We do not know how many greeted him – perhaps just a few of his followers and the odd bystander seeking some entertainment, or perhaps the hundreds or thousands traditionally imagined. We do know that at Passover, with the city overflowing with tens of thousands of pilgrims united not just in their love of God but their hatred of Rome, tensions were high and the potential for riots ever-present. No wonder the Romans were keen to clamp down on any hint of public disorder.

But *Ride* on attempts to capture not a historical event so much as a theological one. Henry Hart Milman, the author (1791-1868) was a clergyman, a very considerable classical scholar and Dean of St Paul's. In his mind, the triumphal entry is the first act of a drama, which will end in victory. The two are inseparable: Christ rides on in majesty, unquestionably the King, but he 'In lowly pomp rides on to die.' But from the perspective of history, he is already victorious: 'O Christ, your triumphs now begin/ O'er captive death and conquered sin.' The triumphal entry is not just ironic and pathetic, even though his disciples will all forsake him and flee: Jesus really is the King. And, as Milman says, 'your last and fiercest strife is nigh' – the crucifixion – and it is on the other side of this painful death that 'The Father on his sapphire throne/ Awaits his own anointed Son.'

So for Milman, Jesus is doing battle with sin and death, and the triumphal entry is the beginning of the fight, like a boxer advancing to the ring. It is a wonderful image, and a true perception which enriches our understanding of the story.

In the UK, *Ride on* is usually sung to *Winchester New*, a German tune from 1690 harmonised by William Monk, who was the first musical editor for the hugely influential *Hymns Ancient and Modern* and wrote *Eventide*, the tune to *Abide with me*. He smoothed out the rhythms of many of the old dance tunes to which the hymns were set, making them singable by respectable congregations and a little dull. Thomas Hardy wrote of hymns which were:

'Stripped of some of your vesture
By Monk or another. Now you wore no frill,
And at first you startled me. But I know you still,
Though I missed the minim's waver
And the dotted quaver.'

Nowadays some of the originals are being recovered and given a new lease of life. Maddy Prior and the Carnival Band recorded 18th century hymns for a revelatory album called *Sing Lustily and with Good Courage* in 1990, which is still available.

Rock of ages, cleft for me,
 Let me hide myself in thee;
Let the water and the blood,
From thy riven side which flowed,
Be of sin the double cure;
Save me from its guilt and power.

Not the labour of my hands
Can fulfill thy law's demands;
Could my zeal no respite know,
Could my tears forever flow,
All for sin could not atone;
Thou must save, and thou alone.

Nothing in my hand I bring,
Simply to thy cross I cling;
Naked, come to thee for dress;
Helpless look to thee for grace;
Foul, I to the fountain fly;
Wash me, Saviour, or I die.

While I draw this fleeting breath,
When mine eyes shall close in death,
When I soar to worlds unknown,
See thee on thy judgement throne,
Rock of ages, cleft for me,
Let me hide myself in thee.

Rock of ages

NEAR the Somerset village of Blagdon, visitors to the picturesque ravine of Burrington Coombe are shown the place where one of the most famous hymns in the language was composed while its author was sheltering from a thunderstorm.

Historians are at odds with the local tourist board and think it was composed somewhere else entirely: but *Rock of ages* and Burrington Coombe are inextricably linked. Perhaps it is not as far-fetched as all that. Augustus Montague Toplady (1740-1778), the author, was curate of Blagdon, and we are free to believe in a literal rock if we like.

However, for Toplady it was the eternal Rock of salvation that was important. Born in Surrey and educated at Westminster College and Trinity College, Dublin, Toplady was converted by a follower of John Wesley preaching in a barn in County Wexford. Wesley was an Arminian, believing in the free grace of God available to all; Toplady became a convinced Calvinist, believing in predestination and the absolute sovereignty of God. It was not a sensitive age, and their differing theologies led to a protracted and bitter public controversy in which neither showed himself in a very good light.

Rock of ages, for all its explicit Calvinism, transcends party spirit – so much so that it finds a place in the new Methodist hymn book, *Singing the Faith*. Perhaps this is an indication that both Calvinists and Arminians, while they might disagree about how grace works, are united in their grasp of its centrality to our understanding of God. We do not get what we deserve; we cannot earn our own salvation; God is love, and all good things come from him.

The title of the hymn is a reference to the story of Moses in Exodus, where he asks to see God's face and is refused. However, God says that 'while my glory passes by I will put you in a cleft of the rock, and I will cover you with my hand until I have passed by' (33. 22). There are other places where God is referred to as a 'rock' in the Old Testament. 2 Samuel 22. 2-3 says: 'The Lord is my rock and my fortress and my deliverer, my God, my rock, in whom I take refuge,' while Psalm 61. 2 says: 'From the end of the earth I call to you when my heart is faint. Lead me to the rock that is higher than I.' In 1 Corinthians 10. 4 Christ is referred to as a rock; 'cleft for me' alludes then to his crucifixion.

The rest of the hymn is a heartfelt appeal to God's grace and mercy, and a restatement of Toplady's Calvinist theology. Interestingly, his first version read 'Be of sin the double cure, Save from wrath, and make me pure' – Wesley's doctrine of Christian perfection, perhaps, in which the 'double cure' is salvation by the atonement and strength to live a sinless life. Later editions referred to the 'guilt and power' of sin.

The second verse is stark in its denial of all human capacity for salvation. 'Not the labour of my hands/ Can fulfill thy laws demands …'

The theme continues in the third: 'Nothing in my hand I bring/ Simply to thy cross I cling.' The great Baptist preacher C H Spurgeon was fond of quoting this, particularly at the beginning of his ministry. A little too fond: a waspish well-wisher used to send him critiques of his sermons, once remarking: 'We are sufficiently informed of the vacuity of your hands.'

The last verse is sublime. It imagines the flight of the soul through 'tracts' or 'worlds' unknown to God, where he is seated in judgment. The cloven Rock is there as a shelter from the greatest storm of all, however, and he is safe.

Arguably Toplady's vision is flawed at this point. He seems to think of a wrathful God the Father, and Christ as counsel for the defence, or as a safe room as protection against divine violence. We would not put it in this way today, but there is great power in this image of Christ as a refuge from the storm, and the ultimate guarantor of our place in heaven.

Tell out, my soul, the greatness of the Lord!
Unnumbered blessings give my spirit voice;
tender to me the promise of his word;
in God my Saviour shall my heart rejoice.

Tell out, my soul

TIMOTHY Dudley-Smith is one of our very best modern hymn-writers, with a great gift for verse which is biblical and deeply spiritual.

Tell out, my soul is probably his most popular piece. Ironically, it does not display his hymn-writing talents to the full; it is not much more than a versification of a Bible passage (Luke 1. 46-55). But even in this, there is very considerable skill.

He has thought deeply about the passage, and using many of the original expressions in the text he has brought its themes together in a traditional verse form. Each stanza is a call to 'Tell out, my soul, the greatness' – of the Lord, his Name, his Might and his Word, and the hymn reaches a soaring climax as we sing, 'Tell out my soul, the greatness of the Lord/ To children's children and for evermore!' Sung either at the beginning or the end of worship, it is a wonderful expression of praise.

It is, though, more than that, as the author knew very well. Mary's song, the 'Magnificat' (from the first word in Latin) is a song of revolution. God is on the side of the poor and powerless. 'He has scattered those who are proud in their inmost thoughts, he has brought down rulers from their thrones, but has lifted up the humble. He has filled the hungry with good things, but the rich he has sent empty away.'

At different times and in different places in the life of God's people, this has been a dangerous song to sing, and Christians have suffered for it. We should not sing it today without realising what it means, and being honest about our own situations.

We may need to realise that we are the rich and powerful of the world, compared with those who have nothing.

But we may need to be comforted if we are facing injustice ourselves, at work or in the home, perhaps. Knowing that God is for us helps us face whatever life can throw at us.

There are other themes here, too: confidence in God's grace, and awareness of weakness and sin, but these are all held together by the same call to 'tell out the greatness' of God and what he has done. Mary's song, and our hymn, are profound expressions of faith in God, who never abandons us, and in whom there is always a future and a hope.

Timothy Dudley-Smith was ordained a priest in the Church of England in 1951 and retired as Bishop of Thetford in 1992.

Tell out, my soul is often sung to *Woodlands*, by Walter Greatorex. He was music master at Gresham's School in Holt, Norfolk, England, from 1911 to 1949.

The day thou gavest, Lord, is ended,
The darkness falls at thy behest;
To thee our morning hymns ascended,
Thy praise shall sanctify our rest.

We thank thee that thy church, unsleeping,
While earth rolls onward into light,
Through all the world her watch is keeping,
And rests not now by day or night.

As o'er each continent and island
The dawn leads on another day,
The voice of prayer is never silent,
Nor dies the strain of praise away.

The sun that bids us rest is waking
Our brethren 'neath the western sky,
And hour by hour fresh lips are making
Thy wondrous doings heard on high.

So be it, Lord; thy throne shall never,
Like earth's proud empires, pass away:
Thy kingdom stands, and grows forever,
Till all thy creatures own thy sway.

The day thou gavest, Lord, is ended

EVENING services are growing fewer in British churches, with many abandoning them or holding them monthly as the emphasis moves to family-friendly church. This is understandable, but it means that a distinctive layer of spirituality is less accessible to younger generations. Evening services are often quieter and more reflective. They do not try to stir our emotions so much as to help us rest in the presence of God and lay hold of his promises for the coming week.

The day thou gavest, Lord has been an integral part of this evening spirituality since its first publication in 1870. John Ellerton (1826-1893), an Anglican clergyman and authority on hymnology who composed more than 80 hymns, wrote it as part of a service entitled 'A Liturgy for Missionary Meetings'. Its missionary impetus breathes through every verse.

Its premise is very simple, but Ellerton makes it something profound. As the world turns, it is always dusk somewhere and dawn somewhere else. Everywhere in the world, as one part of the Church is bringing its daily prayers to a close, another part is beginning them. God is praised all over the world, always.

Ellerton expresses this simple truth in calm, dignified language which rises to the level of poetry – and not all his hymns do, by any means. Of the many he wrote – all of them accomplished verse and theologically sensible – this is the one which most touches the heart and seizes the imagination.

> *As o'er each continent and island*
> *The dawn leads on another day,*
> *The voice of prayer is never silent,*
> *Nor dies the strain of praise away.*

We can see it; he has made geography spiritual.

At one level, we need to appreciate this hymn for its own sake. Our Christian faith started with twelve apostles at Pentecost, a tiny number to pit against a hostile world. But they were filled with the Holy Spirit and they had seen the risen Lord Jesus, and now the Church is in every country in the world, in vast numbers. Our relative decline in Europe is more than offset by the surge in the global South, and now 'reverse missionaries' are making an impact even in the UK as daughter churches support their mother. 'The sun that bids us rest is waking/ Our brethren 'neath the western sky ...' This is a cause for praise and thanksgiving; it makes us lift our eyes from our limited horizons and local difficulties, and gives us a vision of a greater God.

But it's also helpful for us to see the hymn in its context. Ellerton lived at a time when the British Empire was enjoying unchallenged global domination. Every year saw new territories added. Many saw it as a great force for good, and believed that the Empire was God's instrument to civilise the world. His 'brethren 'neath the western sky' were the

Anglo-Saxon nations of the US and Canada, and beyond them the British-held territories of the Pacific, India and Africa.

Yet in spite of these imperialist overtones, he finishes his hymn on a note of humility: 'So be it, Lord; thy throne shall never,/ Like earth's proud empires, pass away ...' Even Britain's vast empire would not last, but God's would stand and grow forever, 'Till all thy creatures own thy sway.'

That humility was echoed by no less a person than Queen Victoria, who chose it to be sung at her Diamond Jubilee celebrations in 1897. It was also sung when Britain returned control of Hong Kong to China in 1997. All human empires fall; only God's is eternal.

The light of the morning is breaking,
The shadows are passing away;
The nations of earth are awaking,
New peoples are learning to pray.
Let wrong, O Redeemer, be righted,
In knowing and doing thy will;
And gather, as brothers united,
All men to thy cross on the hill.

The light of the morning is breaking

WALES has given the world more great hymns than most other nations, punching far above its weight for its small size. Not for nothing is it called the land of song, and singing a good Welsh hymn to a good Welsh tune can be a thrilling experience.

Many of these hymns are from Nonconformist writers – the established Church has never been strong in Wales – but they have enriched the whole Church of God.

The light of the morning is breaking is by Howell Elvet Lewis (1860-1953), a Congregational minister whose long life spanned the great period of Welsh Nonconformity. The title is from Isaiah 58. 8, which in the Authorized Version reads: 'Then shall thy light break forth as the morning, and thine health shall spring forth speedily: and thy righteousness shall go before thee; the glory of the LORD shall be thy reward.'

The hymn's three verses reflect a passion for justice alongside a firm theological conviction that it is God, not human beings, who will establish an eternal kingdom of righteousness, peace and love. Lewis is optimistic: 'The nations of earth are awaking,/New peoples are learning to pray', but this vision of 'one family united' will only come to pass through God's gracious action.

In verse 2 he says, 'Your pity alone can deliver/ The earth from her sorrows, dear Lord/ Her pride and her hardness forgive her/ Your blood for her ransom was poured.'

Lewis was true to a biblical insight which was often overlooked in his day, as it is in ours: that the Christian hope is in what God will do, not in what we can do. In theological language, it is 'eschatological'. He looks forward to the time when 'Your throne, great Redeemer, be founded/ In radiance of wisdom and love', and ends with an echo of Psalm 46:

> *Though hills and high mountains should tremble,*
> *Though all that is seen melt away,*
> *Your voice shall in triumph assemble*
> *Your loved ones at dawning of day.*

But his echo of Isaiah 58 is deliberate, too. The promise in that chapter that 'your light will break forth like the dawn' is conditional: the chapter as a whole is a fierce attack on the hypocrisy of God's people who are externally religious but practise injustice. God will bless those who do right, not those who only talk about it.

Elvet Lewis was born in Carmarthenshire, the eldest of 12 children of James and Anna Lewis. His father was a farm labourer and there was little money in the family, but they managed to send him to a grammar school when he was 14. He began to preach, and while still a teenager went to Carmarthen Presbyterian College to train for ministry.

Throughout a long ministry in Wales and in England (notably at Tabernacle, King's Cross, for 36 years) he maintained a deep love of the Welsh language and literature. He wrote poems, essays and hymns in Welsh, and received academic as well as popular acclaim: he was honoured by the University of Wales with three degrees, and made Companion of Honour by George VI.

Among other books he wrote *Sweet Singers of Wales*, with biographies of hymn writers and translations of their hymns, available free online.

The light of the morning is breaking is sung to *Crugybar,* a Welsh traditional melody.

There's a light upon the mountains,
* And the day is at the spring,*
When our eyes shall see the beauty
And the glory of the King:
Weary was our heart with waiting,
And the night watch seemed so long,
But his triumph day is breaking
And we hail it with a song.

In the fading of the starlight
We may see the coming morn;
And the lights of men are paling
In the splendours of the dawn;
For the eastern skies are glowing
As with light of hidden fire,
And the hearts of men are stirring
With the throbs of deep desire.

There's a hush of expectation
And a quiet in the air
And the breath of God is moving
In the fervent breath of prayer;
For the suffering, dying Jesus
Is the Christ upon the throne,
And the travail of our spirit
Is the travail of his own.

He is breaking down the barriers,
He is casting up the way;
He is calling for his angels
To break ope the gates of day:
But his angels here are human,
Not the shining hosts above;
For the drum beats of his army
Are the heartbeats of our love.

Hark! we hear a distant music
And it comes with fuller swell;
'Tis the triumph song of Jesus,
Of our King, Immanuel!
Go ye forth with joy to meet him!
And, my soul, be swift to bring
All thy sweetest and thy dearest
For the triumph of our King!

✜

There's a light upon the mountain

THIS great Nonconformist Advent hymn is a stirring call to spiritual battle. It is soaked in scripture, but it never loses sight of the real world in which we who sing it have to live. It has rousing, memorable lines, but there is a clear theological progression through it, and it ends exactly where the writer wants it to be.

Henry Burton (1940-1930) lived most of his long life in England as a Wesleyan Methodist minister, though he was educated in America; his parents emigrated there from Leicestershire when he was young, but he returned to England in his 20s. He ministered in Lancashire and London and wrote several hymns, of which this is the best-known.

Advent is the time to remember the coming of Christ into the world, and it is traditionally linked with his Second Coming. This is the theme of *There's a light upon the mountain*. The line 'and the day is at the spring' in the first verse echoes Zechariah's words in Luke 1. 78, when his son John the Baptist was born. 'Weary was our heart with waiting' is a reference to the aged Simeon and Anna, who recognised the infant Christ when he was presented in the Temple.

The second verse draws a picture of the world before Jesus was born, longing for the coming Messiah. The failure of human endeavours to create a better world are contrasted with the coming Kingdom: 'the lights of men are paling in the splendours of the dawn'. The coming of the Magi is referred to in the lines 'For the eastern skies are glowing as with light of hidden fire.'

In the third verse the focus moves from the birth of Jesus to his death, resurrection and glorification: 'the suffering, dying Jesus is the Christ upon the throne'. This is the bridge to the next section, which speaks of his continuing ministry through his Church. The language is taken from Isaiah 40. 3 – 'he is breaking down the barriers, he is casting up the way'. The picture is of a triumphant, unstoppable royal progress. A new world is coming into being, the Kingdom of God; but it is built by his people, as the disciples of Christ act as salt and light in a dark world. 'But his angels here are human, not the shining hosts above ...'

In the last verse the note of triumph sounds even more loudly, as the hymn-writer looks forward to the completion of God's plans for his creation. He has in mind the words of the Psalmist about the Hebrew kings, and John's visions in Revelation: the Old Testament is fulfilled in the new, and one day every knee shall bow and every tongue confess that Jesus is Lord.

The scripture themes in the hymn are implicit, rather than being spelt out. We have to work a little harder to understand its flow. But its denser texture adds to its value as poetry, and it is a richly meaningful meditation on the Advent theme.

There's a wideness in God's mercy,
Like the wideness of the sea;
There's a kindness in his justice,
Which is more than liberty.

There is no place where earth's sorrows
Are more felt than up in heaven;
There is no place where earth's failings
Have such kindly judgement given.

For the love of God is broader
Than the measure of our mind;
And the heart of the Eternal
Is most wonderfully kind.

But we make his love too narrow
By false limits of our own;
And we magnify his strictness
With a zeal he will not own.

There is plentiful redemption
In the blood that has been shed;
There is joy for all the members
In the sorrows of the head.

If our love were but more simple,
We should take him at his word;
And our lives would be all sunshine
In the sweetness of our Lord.

There's a wideness in God's mercy

ONE of the movements which most influenced the current of religious affairs in the 19th century was the High Church revival known as the Oxford Movement. Strictly speaking it lasted from 1833-45, from the

Assize sermon preached by John Keble to the reception of John Henry Newman into the Roman Catholic Church. It is hard at this distance in time, and in such a different world, to imagine the power of those events to shock. Neverthless, at the time the country talked of little else. The Church of England was in crisis as some of its best and brightest concluded that it was not a true Church at all, and that Rome was right all along.

One of those who was swept along by the influence of Newman was Frederick William Faber. He was a very promising and talented young man, though prone to enthusiasms. He became a scholar, an Anglican clergyman and a friend of the poet Wordsworth, but followed Newman into the Roman Catholic Church in 1845. He founded the Brompton Oratory but died at the age of only 49, having had years of ill-health.

He wrote three volumes of hymns, mainly because the translations of Catholic hymns from the continent which were sung in British Catholic churches had too much of a foreign feel: 'They do not express Saxon thoughts and feelings, and consequently the poor do not seem to take to them,' he said in the preface to one of them. One of his suggested replacements is *There's a wideness in God's mercy*. It is a remarkable hymn in many ways, with some very striking verses, along with some lines that are not very good. The versions sung in most churches today are almost always shorter than Faber's original and the order of the verses varies. Interestingly in one omitted verse, meditating on the extent of God's love and power, he contemplates life on other planets:

> *There is grace enough for thousands*
> *Of new worlds as great as this;*
> *There is room for fresh creations*
> *In that upper home of bliss.*

Above all, though, the hymn is notable for its passionate plea for an understanding of God's grace:

> *For the love of God is broader*
> *Than the measure of man's mind;*
> *And the heart of the eternal*
> *Is most wonderfully kind.*

Faber wrote those line against the background of the really bitter theological controversies of his day, when Protestants and Catholics could find nothing good to say about each other and there was a deep hostility between them – and between the various Protestant sects as well. His words, too, might well have been aimed at the respectable middle classes who condemned the poor for their fecklessness and chaotic lifestyles instead of trying to understand them and help. It might be thought that not much has changed.

The fourth verse says:

> *But we make his love too narrow*
> *By false limits of our own;*
> *And we magnify his strictness*
> *With a zeal he will not own*

– own in the sense of 'acknowledge'.

It is surprising, to say the least, to find a senior Roman Catholic clergyman writing such words in the middle of the 19th century. Faber was by no stretch of the imagination a theological liberal, but he had an intuitive sense that God was bigger than any human understanding. As someone who had taken the enormously costly decision to turn his back on the faith of his forefathers (his ancestors had been Protestant Huguenots who had fled persecution in France), he was well aware that truth mattered. Nevertheless, he says, God is the judge, and we should be as charitable and patient as we can.

The usual last verse is rather feeble – 'If our love were but more simple,/ We should take him at his word' – but it expresses Faber's mind and character very well. He was not a great theologian, but he understood very well that God is more interested in the sort of person we are than the sort of things we know.

Through the love of God our Saviour,
All will be well;
Free and changeless is his favour;
All, all is well.
Precious is the blood that healed us;
Perfect is the grace that sealed us;
Strong the hand stretched out to shield us;
All must be well.

Though we pass through tribulation,
All will be well;
Ours is such a full salvation;
All, all is well.
Happy still in God confiding,
Fruitful, if in Christ abiding,
Holy through the Spirit's guiding,
All must be well.

We expect a bright tomorrow;
All will be well;
Faith can sing through days of sorrow,
All, all is well.
On our Father's love relying,
Jesus every need supplying,
Or in living, or in dying,
All must be well.

Through the love of God our Saviour

THERE are a few hymns which marry words and music perfectly. *Through the love of God our Saviour* is not always sung to *Ar Hyd Y Nos (All through the night)* but it arguably should be: there is a perfect match between the simple but sonorous verses and the strong but delicate cadences of the music.

The hymn was composed by Mary Peters (1813-1856), a writer whose other work is not much known. This hymn has survived because it is absolutely perfect of its type: simple enough, but profound and technically excellent – all those feminine rhymes (with the rhyme on the penultimate syllable, as in confiding/abiding/guiding) are not easy to pull off. There are phrases that stick in the mind and ring true to our experience.

It begins with an affirmation of faith in God, his free gift of salvation through the death of Jesus and his everlasting care for those who have accepted him. 'All will be well' not because of anything we achieve or any security we obtain, but because of the grace of God.

'Though we pass through tribulation/ All will be well: but 'well' in this case is a long way from the sort of prosperity preaching heard sometimes today. She rests her confidence in salvation, not in material wellbeing. 'Wellness' is to be happy, fruitful and holy, through faith in God.

The final verse looks forward to the 'bright tomorrow' which awaits the disciples of Christ. 'Faith can sing through days of sorrow' – whatever dark valleys we go through in this life, there is always hope for the future. She concludes: 'Or [in the sense of "whether"] in living, or in dying,/ All must be well.'

The repeated refrain echoes Julian of Norwich, the mediaeval mystic, who wrote 'All shall be well, and all shall be well, and all manner of thing shall be well' – lines taken up by T S Eliot in *Little Gidding*, the last of the *Four Quartets*. She may have read Julian, though in some ways it would be unlikely.

Mary Peters was born Mary Bowly in Cirencester, Gloucestershire. Her father Richard was a linen draper and a member of a well-known Quaker family in the town.

At the age of 39 – and after she had written most of her hymns – she married John Peters, formerly Rector of Quenington in Gloucestershire and a widower. (A story that she married and was widowed young appears to be untrue.) Peters had acquired Nonconformist principles, resigned his living and built a chapel in Quenington, probably affiliated with the Plymouth Brethren; it is said that George Muller, the famous Bristol philanthropist and member of the Brethren, conducted their wedding in Cirencester.

Shortly after the marriage they moved to Clifton in Bristol and lived happily together until Mary's death four years later at the age of 43. She is buried in Arnos Vale Cemetery there.

Through the love of God our Saviour is the only one of her hymns to be widely sung now, but it is worth saying that Frances Ridley Havergal praised them. 'Calmer, riper and maturer are the hymns of Mary Bowly,' she said. 'They are not the hymns of a young Christian, but evidently of one who has found "grace for grace" and gone from "strength to strength". Every line, generally speaking, contains some distinct reality of Scripture truth or Christian experience. The bright assurance of faith is expressed in these hymns with the simple, absolute rest of the soul in the infinite and absolute love of the Father in His Son, Jesus Christ.'

*W*e come unto our fathers' God,
　　Their rock is our salvation;
Th'eternal arms, their dear abode,
We make our habitation.
We bring thee, Lord, the praise they brought,
We seek thee as thy saints have sought
In every generation.

The fire divine their steps that led
Still goeth bright before us;
The heavenly shield around them spread
Is still high holden o'er us;
The grace those sinners that subdued,
The strength those weaklings that renewed,
Doth vanquish, doth restore us.

Their joy unto their Lord we bring,
Their song to us descendeth;
The Spirit who in them did sing
To us his music lendeth;
His song in them, in us, is one;
We raise it high, we send it on—
The song that never endeth.

Ye saints to come, take up the strain,
The same sweet theme endeavour;
Unbroken be the golden chain!
Keep on the song forever!
Safe in the same dear dwelling place,
Rich with the same eternal grace,
Bless the same boundless giver.

We come unto our fathers' God

FAMILY history is increasingly popular, even more so as the internet has made research so much easier than it used to be. Many of us enjoy trawling the archives for clues about how our ancestors lived, what they thought and how they felt.

We are less interested in Church history, generally speaking, but arguably these spiritual ancestors of ours are even more important. They left us the buildings, the songs, the prayers and the habits of mind which make us the Christians we are today.

There is a story about a young preacher who came to a church which had just a few in the congregation. He remarked on the emptiness of the pews to an old deacon, who said: 'What do you mean, empty? The church is full.' He told the young man about all those who over the years had built the church, prayed, witnessed and loved it. 'They are all still here. It is called the communion of saints!'

This sense of connection with those who have gone before is very precious, and it is expressed in a hymn by the wonderfully-named Thomas Hornblower Gill (1819-1906), *We come unto our fathers' God*.

Gill came from a Presbyterian family that had turned Unitarian, as many did, but found his way to evangelical doctrines through the hymns of Isaac Watts, whose deep feeling contrasted with the chilly intellectualism of the Unitarian faith. He wrote around 200 hymns which were widely sung and highly regarded, though this is one of the very few still to be in regular use today. One commentator described him as 'a more intellectual Charles Wesley'. He lived the quiet and retired life of a private scholar; one would-be biographer says that 'his life has been singularly devoid of outward incident'.

He printed his hymns in a compilation, *The Golden Chain*, first published in 1869. He writes of *We come unto our fathers' God:*

'The birthday of this hymn, November 22nd, 1868 (St Cecelia's Day), was almost the most delightful day of my life. Its production employed the whole day and was a prolonged rapture ... It was produced while the *Golden Chain* was being printed, just in time to be a link therein, and was the latest, as *How, Lord, shall vows of ours be sweet?* was the earliest song included therein.'

It is fitting that the last verse includes the lines 'Unbroken be the golden chain!/ Keep on the song forever!'

The theme of the hymn is the continuity of the Church of today with the Church of yesterday, and indeed of centuries ago: 'We bring thee, Lord, the praise they brought,/ We seek thee as thy saints have sought/ In every generation.'

But Gill is not interested in theological questions like the apostolic succession or the right mode of baptism; he does not want to establish this continuity to score points, as many in that age of controversy did. Instead, he sees it as a promise of blessing for the future. God has kept his people in the past, and we should not doubt that he will continue to do so. 'The fire divine their steps that led/ Still goeth bright before us';

> *Their joy unto their Lord we bring,*
> *Their song to us descendeth;*
> *The Spirit who in them did sing*
> *To us his music lendeth.*

Above all, it is a message of encouragement: we can learn faith from those who have gone before us.

Gill's outward life seems to have been unexciting. His inner life, though, was very rich, and many of his hymns show evidence of deep reflection on spiritual things; perhaps more of them should be recovered.

When I survey the wondrous cross
On which the prince of glory died,
My richest gain I count but loss,
And pour contempt on all my pride.

Forbid it, Lord, that I should boast,
Save in the death of Christ my God!
All the vain things that charm me most,
I sacrifice them to his blood.

See from his head, his hands, his feet,
Sorrow and love flow mingled down!
Did e'er such love and sorrow meet,
Or thorns compose so rich a crown?

Were the whole realm of nature mine,
That were an offering far too small;
Love so amazing, so divine,
Demands my soul, my life, my all.

When I survey the wondrous cross

WHEN I survey the wondrous cross is the purest and most deeply-felt of all devotional hymns, and it has an honoured place in Christian worship.

Originally written in preparation for a communion service in 1707, it was at first called 'Crucifixion to the World by the Cross of Christ', and had five stanzas. The fourth, which Watts put in brackets indicating that it could be left out if need be, read:

His dying crimson, like a robe,
Spreads o'er his body on the tree:
Then am I dead to all the globe,
And all the globe is dead to me.

His guess was probably right – the words are not sung now. Perhaps the image of the blood of the crucified Christ covering him like an Emperor's cloak is just too shocking for modern tastes.

The original words of the hymn have been altered plenty of times, sometimes by the author. He originally wrote 'Where the young Prince of Glory died' in the first verse; now it is often 'On which the Prince of Glory died'. The revision is better, as the stress falls on a weak word when it is sung.

When this hymn was written, congregational singing was limited to the Psalms, if that; early Dissenters – Baptists, Congregationalists and the like – had fierce controversies over whether hymn-singing was permitted at all. Isaac Watts, because his hymns were so firmly rooted in the Bible, helped to make the practice acceptable.

Interestingly, *When I survey* is the first hymn we know of to be written in the first person. Its author is not trying to teach doctrine; the hymn is a profound response to what Christ has done for us, and a moving evocation of the cost of salvation.

It is a particularly appropriate hymn to sing at Communion, where at the Lord's Table we are asked to examine ourselves before we eat and drink, and to be at peace with God and one another. 'My richest gain I count but loss, and pour contempt on all my pride' in the sight of the Cross. We see the empty riches of the world for what they are, and leave them all for him – 'sacrifice them to his blood'.

In the third verse there is an astonishing imaginative insight, which stretches language to express the inexpressible. It is not blood which flows from Christ's wounds, but sorrow and love; the linkage recalls the water – the pericardial fluid – and blood which flowed from his side. In the third line sorrow and love have reverted to their natural meanings – they are both seen at their most extreme in the suffering of Christ. But when we 'see' his blood, that is what we are seeing; again, it is an intensification of our experience at Communion. The crown of thorns goes with the cloak of blood in the excluded fourth verse.

Extreme love calls for an extreme response: 'love so amazing, so divine, demands my soul, my life, my all'.

Where cross the crowded ways of life,
Where sound the cries of race and clan
Above the noise of selfish strife,
We hear thy voice, O Son of Man.

In haunts of wretchedness and need,
On shadowed thresholds dark with fears,
From paths where hide the lures of greed,
We catch the vision of thy tears.

The cup of water given for thee,
Still holds the freshness of thy grace;
Yet long these multitudes to view
The sweet compassion of thy face.

O Master, from the mountainside
Make haste to heal these hearts of pain;
Among these restless throngs abide;
O tread the city's streets again.

Till humankind shall learn thy love
And follow where thy feet have trod,
Till, glorious from thy heaven above,
Shall come the city of our God!

Where cross the crowded ways of life

'GOD made the country, and man made the town' is nowadays a rather old-fashioned way of looking at the world. We want to celebrate the good things about cities. Today most people do live there, and it would be sad if all we thought about was getting out of them.

There are still places in our cities, though – in any city – which are dark, bleak and cold. They crush the spirit, and those who live there do so because they have no other choice.

Frank Mason North (1850-1935) was a Methodist minister in New York, a good pastor and a talented administrator who was respected in his denomination. But the New York of his day was a bustling, heaving, growing city, where the relentless quest of money left many casualties behind it. There was mass immigration, often of the poorest Europeans seeking a better life. Even the prosperous middle classes who made up the respectable churchgoers of Frank Mason North's world did not have to go very far to find the most desperate want.

North, though, refused to close his eyes to the needs of the poor. He wrote *Where cross the crowded ways of life* in 1903: the 'crowded ways' were the streets and alleys of New York, riven by competing interests, ethnic tensions and the struggle for survival: 'where sound the cries of race and clan' as the hymn says.

But there is nowhere beyond the reach of Christ – or of his Church:

> *In haunts of wretchedness and need,*
> *On shadowed thresholds dark with fears,*
> *From paths where hide the lures of greed,*
> *We catch the vision of your tears.*

He draws on Matthew 10. 42 in his next verse: 'And if anyone gives even a cup of cold water to one of these little ones who is my disciple, truly I tell you, that person will certainly not lose their reward.'

> *The cup of water given for you*
> *Still holds the freshness of your grace;*
> *Yet long these multitudes to view*
> *The sweet compassion of your face.*

There is, he is saying, something more than meeting physical needs: people need to meet with the living Christ themselves, and see him face to face.

He also draws on the story of the Transfiguration in Matthew 17 and Mark 9. Jesus goes up onto a mountain with three of his disciples and meets Moses and Elijah; when he comes down his other disciples are struggling with a case of demon-possession, and he has to heal the boy himself. So, the hymn says:

> *O Master, from the mountainside*
> *Make haste to heal these hearts of pain;*
> *Among these restless throngs abide;*
> *O tread the city's streets again.*

There is only so much we can do; we need the help of Christ himself.

North would go on to campaign against the hideous conditions under which labourers, including children, had to suffer. Churches received significant financial support from mill and mine owners, and it was in their interest to ignore the squalid transactions that produced the wealth from which they benefited. As chair of an ecumenical committee he was responsible for a highly influential report, *The Church in the Modern World,* in whose preface he wrote: 'Rich and poor, capitalist and labouring man, are not classifications and distinctions made by the Church of Christ.'

For all his commitment to making life better for the poor in this world, he always had his eyes focused on Christ, and on his ultimate victory: 'Till glorious from your heaven above/ Shall come the city of our God.'

Who would true valour see
Let him come hither;
One here will constant be,
Come wind, come weather.
There's no discouragement,
Shall make him once relent,
His first avowed intent,
To be a pilgrim.

Who so beset him round,
With dismal stories,
Do but themselves confound;
His strength the more is.
No lion can him fright,
He'll with a giant fight,
But he will have a right,
To be a pilgrim.

Hobgoblin, nor foul fiend,
Can daunt his spirit:
He knows, he at the end,
Shall life inherit.
Then fancies fly away,
He'll fear not what men say,
He'll labour night and day,
To be a pilgrim.

Who would true valour see

THERE are not many figures in Church history who have given as much to us in one book as John Bunyan.

The Pilgrim's Progress was published in two parts, in 1678 and 1684, and it has shaped the way we think about our Christian discipleship ever since. Discipleship is a journey; conversion is the first step, but there are many trials and tribulations to face on the way to the Celestial City.

We will be attacked, by the Giant Despair, Apollyon and all manner of enemies. We will fall into the Slough of Despond, we will go through the Valley of the Shadow of Death, we will be waylaid in Vanity Fair. But we will find help along the way from Valiant-for-Truth and Greatheart, and if we remain faithful we will arrive at our destination.

Part of the charm of the book is that Bunyan's pilgrims are not spiritual supermen. They are like us, and like us they sing to keep their spirits up. One of those songs has become a classic hymn, known and loved all over the world.

Who would true valour see is a vivid portrayal of the perils of the journey. Bunyan's original version speaks of wind and weather, wild animals, giants, and spiritual forces. But 'hobgoblin nor foul fiend/ Can daunt his spirit', because 'he knows he at the end/ Shall life inherit'.

This hymn is a great statement of faith, and a call to have courage. It is also a radical call to discipleship. Life, says Bunyan, is not random. It has a purpose, and everything that happens – illness, opposition, misfortune, comfort, happiness, defeat and victory – is fundamentally spiritual. God is in it, and it is up to us to see his hand at work. If we are faithful, then one day he will bring us home, and all the trials we go through will seem nothing in the light of the glory he has prepared for us.

John Bunyan was a tinker by trade, with very little formal education, though he was a natural writer. In the dark days following the Civil War he was imprisoned because, as a Nonconformist who refused allegiance to the Church of England, he refused to stop holding services and preaching.

He had a vivid sense of the reality of spiritual warfare, but his spirituality was grounded in his experience. When he spoke of being constant 'come wind, come weather', for instance, he was thinking of his rough life as a travelling tinker, but also of the open-air services he and others like him were forced to hold.

The 'dismal stories' he was told may have been the warnings of what would happen if he continued; but 'he'll fear not what men say/ He'll labour night and day/To be a pilgrim'.

Bunyan's plain and forceful style was not well suited to more refined tastes in worship. When Percy Dearmer edited the influential *English Hymnal* in 1906 he smoothed out Bunyan's verse, omitting some of the most vivid lines in favour of more explicit theology. So instead of 'No lion can him fright,' we have 'No foes shall stay his might'; we lose the hobgoblins and foul fiends in favour of 'Since, Lord, thou dost defend/ us with thy Spirit.'

Percy Dearmer was a very good editor, but we are less squeamish about singing Bunyan's original today. We like the honesty and simplicity of what he writes. Lions might very well stand for the sort of enemies we face in our struggles to be a pilgrim. And perhaps – after the horrors of the 20th century, which in 1906 were inconceivable – we are more willing to countenance the reality of spiritual forces of wickedness today.

About the Author

Mark Woods is a Baptist minister who has had pastorates at Downend in Bristol and Alvechurch in Worcestershire. He was editor of *The Baptist Times* and now has a writing ministry which includes serving as consulting editor for the *Methodist Recorder*.